D1606035

HYPER-CALVINISM

THE CALL OF

THE GOSPEL

An Examination of the "Well-Meant Offer" of the Gospel

Revised Edition

David J. Engelsma

REFORMED FREE PUBLISHING ASSOC.
4949 Ivanrest Avenue
Grandville, MI 49418-9709
Phone: (616) 531-1490
Fax: (616) 531-3033

The Reformed Free Publishing Association
Box 2006
Grand Rapids, Michigan 49501

BT
761.2
E 54
1994

ISBN: 0-916206-50-5
Library of Congress: 94-65254

First Edition published 1980

Printed in the United States of America

With gratitude for the instruction of
Herman Hoeksema

Table of Contents

Foreword

This is certainly an interesting, informative, lively, learned discussion of the essence of the gospel call to all mankind. In my opinion, Professor Engelsma carefully defines and convincingly avoids "hyper-Calvinism" himself and clears his denomination, the Protestant Reformed Churches, of so teaching. The locus of the debate among Calvinists concerns what is called "the well-meant offer." Let me locate first what is meant by "well-meant offer" and the area of difference among Calvinists concerning it.

There is much related to this title that is shared by all Calvinists though sometimes differently phrased; namely, that reprobates hear the call and that it is a "serious" call to them. There is one part of the understood meaning of "well-meant offer" that is affirmed by many Calvinists today and denied by others; namely, that God desires and intends the salvation of reprobates in that call they hear or read.

The "well-meant offer" is *understood*, by both sides, to include the notion that *God intends and desires the salvation of reprobates* when the gospel of Jesus Christ is preached to everyone who hears with his ears or reads with his eyes. The late John Murray and Ned B. Stonehouse in *The Free Offer of the Gospel* and the Orthodox Presbyterian Church could declare in 1948 (citing *The Free Offer of the Gospel* by Murray and Stonehouse):

> ...there is in God a benevolent lovingkindness towards the repentance and salvation of even those whom he has not decreed to save. This pleasure, will, *desire* is expressed in the universal call to repentance.... The full and free offer of the gospel is a grace bestowed upon all. Such grace is necessarily a manifestation of love or lovingkindness in the heart of God, and this lovingkindness is revealed to be of a character or kind that is correspondent with the grace bestowed.

The grace offered is nothing less than salvation in its richness and fulness. The love or lovingkindness that lies back of that offer is not anything less; it is the *will to that salvation*. In other words, it is Christ in all the glory of his person and in all the perfection of his finished work whom God offers in the gospel. The loving and benevolent will that is the source of that offer and that grounds its veracity and reality is *the will to the possession of Christ and the enjoyment of the salvation that resides in him* (quoted in **Hyper-Calvinism & the Call of the Gospel**, p. 43).

I have italicized the three statements that *can only mean* in that context that God *desires and intends* ("will" is used on the sense of "intend") the salvation of the reprobates. Much else that is stated *can* be so interpreted but is not unambiguous. All Calvinists (and indeed all Christians) agree that not all human persons are saved. Arminians do champion the notion that God desires and intends the salvation of every person. Calvinists do not, but here Calvinists John Murray, Ned Stonehouse, and the Orthodox Presbyterian Church do so teach.

On the other hand, Herman Hoeksema, the Protestant Reformed denomination, and our author David Engelsma in this book emphatically reject the "well-meant offer" *as including God's desire and intention to save reprobates*.

As a Calvinist, not associated ecclesiastically with the tiny Protestant Reformed denomination and sharply divergent from some of her doctrinal positions, I feel it absolutely necessary to hold with her here where she stands, almost alone today, and suffers massive vituperation and ridicule from Calvinists (no less) for her faithfulness at this point to the gospel of God.

I had the incomparable privilege of being a student of Professors Murray and Stonehouse. With tears in my heart, I nevertheless confidently assert that they erred profoundly in *The Free Offer of the Gospel* and died before they seem to have realized their error which, because of their justifiedly high reputations for Reformed excellence generally, still does incalculable damage to the cause of Jesus Christ and the proclamation of His gospel.

It is absolutely essential to the nature of the only true God and Jesus Christ Whom He has sent that whatever His sovereign majesty desires or intends most certainly — without conceivability of failure in one iota thereof — *must come to pass! Soli Deo Gloria! Amen and amen forevermore! God can never, ever desire or intend **anything** that does not come to pass, or He is not the living, happy God of Abraham, Isaac, and Jacob but an eternally miserable being weeping tears of frustration that He was unable to prevent hell and can never end it thus destroying Himself and heaven in the process.*

"God, the blessed and only Ruler, the King of kings and Lord of lords, who alone is immortal and who lives in unapproachable light, whom no one has seen or can see. To him be honor and might forever. Amen" (1 Tim. 6:15, 16).

JOHN H. GERSTNER
Ligonier, PA

Preface to the Second Edition

The reprinting of *Hyper-Calvinism & the Call of the Gospel* made possible a thorough revision of the book. The revision is much more than merely correcting the "typos" in the first edition or even than including a new "Foreword" by widely known and highly regarded Presbyterian theologian John H. Gerstner.

I have completely reworked the "Introduction"; significantly expanded most of the chapters; and, most importantly, added a new chapter—the fourth in this edition—"Is Denial of the Well-Meant Offer Hyper-Calvinism?"

An effort was made also to enhance the appearance of the book, especially by printing it in larger type.

I take this opportunity to thank Dr. John H. Gerstner for his readiness to grant my request that he write the "Foreword." As those who know him would expect, he has both unerringly called attention to a basic issue in the controversy over the well-meant offer and boldly called for the consistent defense of Calvinism so that this issue is resolved to the glory of God.

This is my purpose and prayer with the reprinting of this book, as I wrote in the preface to the first edition: "God grant that the glorious light of the Reformed faith may shine again and that the darkness of sovereign man and his self-salvation may flee before it."

David J. Engelsma
Grand Rapids, Michigan
June 1993

Preface to the First Edition

Darkness is falling over the Reformed churches in all the world. The light of the Reformed faith is going out. The truth of sovereign, particular grace is lost and with it, the sovereignly gracious God. In the end, Dordt is defeated, and Arminius triumphs.

Yet, we testify of a sovereign God and His sovereign grace in Jesus Christ without pessimism. We know this testimony to be no merely provincial concern — the controversy of a few, small, Reformed denominations. It was the heart of the Reformation; it is the gospel, God's own truth. It shall surely stand. It must be proclaimed. If the children of the Reformation decide now to hold their peace, the stones will immediately cry out.

God grant that the glorious light of the Reformed faith may shine again and that the darkness of sovereign man and his self-salvation may flee before it.

David Engelsma
South Holland, Illinois
September, 1980

Introduction

"Hyper-Calvinism" is a term of reproach and condemnation. It is the charge that a theological teaching which claims to be Calvinism has, in fact, so exaggerated and distorted Calvinism that it is not genuine Calvinism at all. The body of doctrines described as hyper-Calvinism is accused of having gone beyond true Calvinism so that, although it has a semblance of Calvinism, it is in reality a perversion of Calvinism. Indeed, the seriousness of the epithet "hyper-Calvinism" is that it alleges a theological position to be false doctrine.

The fundamental error of hyper-Calvinism is its restriction of the preaching of the gospel. With appeal to the Calvinistic doctrine of divine predestination, it limits the preaching of the gospel to the elect. There may be no bringing of the joyful tidings to all men and women indiscriminately. Especially forbidden is the earnest, urgent call to all men and women without distinction to come to the Savior by believing on Him.

Because the Protestant Reformed Churches in North America reject the well-meant offer of the gospel, these churches are commonly condemned and dismissed in Calvinistic circles as hyper-Calvinists.

This has been the judgment upon the Protestant Reformed Churches by the Christian Reformed Church and her theologians from the beginning of the separate existence of the Protestant Reformed Churches in 1924. Although he did not use the term "hyper-Calvinists," this was the charge against the Protestant Reformed Churches by H.J. Kuiper. Writing at the time of the controversy over common grace that resulted in the formation of the Protestant Reformed Churches, Kuiper declared:

1

One of the most serious aspects of the present denial of the doctrine of Common Grace is the denial of the general offer of salvation. It robs the gospel of its evangelical note. It is bound in time to create an attitude of religious passivism and fatalism which has been the curse of every church where the preaching of election was not counter-balanced by the proclamation of the sinner's responsibility and of God's sincere offer of salvation to all without discrimination.[1]

It was this charge that Herman Hoeksema warded off in his book, *Een Kracht Gods tot Zaligheid of Genade Geen Aanbod (A Power of God unto Salvation or Grace No Offer)*. The editor of the Christian Reformed publication *De Wachter (The Watchman)* was alleging that Hoeksema's rejection of the well-meant offer meant that the gospel should be preached only to the elect. Hoeksema was responding to this allegation when he wrote:

I emphasize, the doctrine (of the well-meant offer, which Hoeksema rejected — DJE) is not that the gospel must be preached *by the preacher* to all men without distinction. But it is that *God Himself* offers His grace to all men and with that, therefore, reveals the earnest desire that it shall be accepted by all.... Our difference, therefore, has absolutely nothing to do with the question whether the gospel must also be preached according to the will of God to all who are in our audience, reprobate as well as elect.[2]

---

1. H.J. Kuiper, *The Three Points of Common Grace* (Grand Rapids: Wm. B. Eerdmans Publishing Co., 1925), p. 13.
2. Herman Hoeksema, *Een Kracht Gods tot Zaligheid of Genade Geen Aanbod* (Grand Rapids: Doorn Printer, 1930), pp. 9, 10, 20. The translation of the Dutch is mine.

Christian Reformed histories invariably present the common grace controversy as the Christian Reformed Church's rejection of hyper-Calvinism.

> There was a deliberate refusal to allow the Arminian overemphasis on common grace to force the Christian Reformed Church to the opposite extreme of denying that grace altogether. One of the accusations against the Rev. Hoeksema... concerned his "insufficient Gospel preaching." The charge was that he preached only for the elect, implicitly denying the sincerity of the Gospel call to the unconverted.... The Christian Reformed Church has found it necessary to guard consistently against a tendency to hyper-orthodoxy by way of reaction against Arminianism.[3]

The official line of the Christian Reformed Church is that she "opposed (the) doctrinal deviation ... (of) hyper-Calvinism in the Common Grace controversy."[4]

This charge against the Protestant Reformed Churches and their theology is spread more widely not only throughout Reformed circles worldwide but also in the broad sphere of evangelical Christianity. Influential Reformed theologian G.C. Berkouwer criticized Herman Hoeksema as a classic hyper-Calvinist:

> It is here that Hoeksema's exegesis of the Canons goes awry, because now the symmetry between election and reprobation becomes a scheme in which the gospel can no longer be truly preached. The missionary mandate, "Make disciples of all the nations" (Matt. 28:19), can no longer function

---

3. John Kromminga, *The Christian Reformed Church: A Study in Orthodoxy* (Grand Rapids: Baker Book House, 1949), pp. 85, 86.
4. Clarence Boomsma, "The CRC: What is Happening to Us?" *Banner* 108 (September 28, 1973), pp. 14, 15.

properly, according to its undeniable emphasis on the purpose of the gospel.... We can no longer speak of glad tidings that go out into the world, except where the gospel reaches the elect. We do not know who they are, but, the purpose of the gospel is twofold: salvation and hardening. The symmetry casts its shadow over the *kerygma*.[5]

Presbyterians are of the same mind and do not hesitate to speak it. In the course of his impassioned defense of a universal love of God in Christ and of a universal will of God unto salvation expressed in the offer of redemption to all men, Scottish Presbyterian theologian Donald Macleod gives a scathing denunciation of the predestinarian theology of Herman Hoeksema: "virtually blasphemous"; "well-nigh blasphemous speculation."[6]

A book circulates among Presbyterians in Australia and New Zealand that is devoted to the refutation of the doctrine of the call of the gospel held by the Protestant Reformed Churches. *Christ Freely Offered* defends the free offer as God's delight in and "pursuit of" the salvation of every sinner (many of whom, however, He fails to catch) and castigates the Protestant Reformed denial of the well-meant offer as hyper-Calvinism.[7]

By the present time, the hyper-Calvinism of Herman Hoeksema and the Protestant Reformed Churches is authoritatively and permanently established in the theological dictionaries. This is enough to daunt all but the hardiest (some would say "foolhardiest") soul! How can one resist the wisdom and power of the dictionaries?

5.   G.C. Berkouwer, *Divine Election,* trans. Hugo Bekker (Grand Rapids: Wm. B. Eerdmans Publishing Co., 1960), p. 223.
6.   Donald Macleod, *Behold Your God* (n.p.:   Christian Focus Publications, 1990), pp. 117-155.
7.   K.W. Stebbins, *Christ Freely Offered: A Discussion of the General Offer of Salvation in the Light of Particular Atonement* (Strathpine North, Australia: Covenanter Press, 1978).

InterVarsity Press has published *The New Dictionary of Theology*. The article on "Hyper-Calvinism" describes the error as emphasizing "irresistible grace to such an extent that there appears to be no real need to evangelize; furthermore, Christ may be offered only to the elect.... It undermines the universal duty of sinners to believe savingly in the Lord Jesus with the assurance that Christ actually died for them." Having described the error, the *Dictionary* confidently identifies the sole modern hyper-Calvinist: "The most prominent recent theologian is the Dutch-American, Herman Hoeksema, in his *Reformed Dogmatics.*"[8]

It came as a shock to the Reformed and evangelical communities, therefore, that the renowned Presbyterian theologian John H. Gerstner recently defended the rejection of the well-meant offer by the Protestant Reformed Churches. In a chapter entitled "Spurious Calvinism" in which he exposes the Arminianism of dispensationalism with regard to every one of the "Five Points of Calvinism," Gerstner subjects the well-meant offer of contemporary Calvinism to searching criticism.

> We must also sadly admit that the majority of Reformed theologians today seriously err concerning the nature of the love of God for reprobates. We mention this here only because this defect in contemporary Reformed theology makes it all the easier for the dispensationalists to continue in their abysmal error.
>
> Most Reformed theologians also include, as a by-product of the Atonement, the well-meant offer of the gospel by which all men can be saved. Some Reformed theologians take a further step still and say that God even intends that they should be saved by this Atonement which

---

8. *New Dictionary of Theology*, ed. Sinclair B. Ferguson, David F. Wright, J.I. Packer (Leicester, England: InterVarsity Press, 1988), pp. 324, 325.

nevertheless was made only for the elect. For example, John Murray and Ned Stonehouse write: "Our Lord ... says expressly that he willed the bestowal of his saving and protecting grace upon those whom neither the Father nor he decreed thus to save and protect." One may sadly say that Westminster Theological Seminary stands for this misunderstanding of the Reformed doctrine since not only John Murray and Ned Stonehouse but also Cornelius VanTil, R.B. Kuiper, John Frame, and, so far as we know, all of the faculty, have favored it. The Christian Reformed Church had already in 1920 taken this sad step away from the Reformed orthodoxy and has been declining ever since. The Presbyterian Church, U.S.A. had even earlier, though somewhat ambiguously, departed and the present mainline Presbyterian church affirms that "The risen Christ is the savior for all men."

The Presbyterian Church in the United States (now part of the Presbyterian Church, U.S.A.) is not far behind, and the separatist Presbyterians such as the Orthodox Presbyterian Church and the Presbyterian Church in America are following in this train. Only the Protestant Reformed Church seems willing to hold to the whole counsel of God on this doctrine.

Gerstner sees the well-meant offer as laying a foundation for "a radical break with the Reformed tradition." The well-meant offer teaches that God is frustrated in His desire to save certain persons. But, says Gerstner, "God, if He could be frustrated in His desires, simply would not be God."[9]

The issue of the well-meant offer is very much alive in Calvinistic circles.

9. John H. Gerstner, *Wrongly Dividing the Word of Truth: A Critique of Dispensationalism* (Brentwood, Tennessee: Wolgemuth & Hyatt, Publishers, Inc., 1991), pp. 125-131.

It is the purpose of this book to show that the rejection of the well-meant offer by the Protestant Reformed Churches is not hyper-Calvinism. This rejection involves no restriction of the promiscuous, lively, urgent preaching of the gospel. It entails no hesitation to call everyone in the preacher's audience to repentance and faith. It originates in no determination to weaken the responsibility of man before the face of the sovereign God.

Rejection of the well-meant offer is pure, sound, consistent Calvinism. It arises out of the Reformed faith itself. It is merely the negative side of the unique Reformed doctrine of the preaching of the gospel as the divine call. It harmonizes perfectly with the other truths of the Reformed faith. Its avowed purpose is the maintenance of the Reformed faith.

The well-meant offer, on the contrary, is not Reformed. It conflicts with basic Reformed truths, notably the truth of predestination. It betrays embarrassment with certain essential doctrines of Calvinism, particularly reprobation. The well-meant offer is, to coin a term, "hypo-Calvinism," that is, a teaching that *falls below* true Calvinism and that works the apostasy from Calvinism of the churches that try to hold the well-meant offer in tension with the "Five Points of Calvinism."

It is also a purpose of this book to give a sharp warning against the real threat of hyper-Calvinism. Some Calvinists have succumbed to hyper-Calvinism. Zealous for the glory of God in the saving of the elect by sovereign grace alone, they denied that the gospel should be preached to all. They specifically denied that the church should call all hearers to faith in the Savior.

It may even be the case that some Reformed and Presbyterian Christians, especially in the British Isles, sincerely confuse the rejection of the well-meant offer by the Protestant Reformed Churches with this genuine hyper-Calvinism. For certain hyper-Calvinists in England spoke of their view as the denial of the offer of salvation.

Hyper-Calvinism is a danger.

It is a danger exactly to the church that embraces the truth of sovereign, particular grace with believing heart by the mighty working of the Spirit of Christ. It is no danger to most churches today. It is no danger to most Reformed and Presbyterian churches today.

The church that confesses sovereign grace must guard against the temptation of restricting the preaching of the gospel: hyper-Calvinism.

The church that confesses sovereign grace must give her defense of sovereign grace in the preaching: the call of the gospel.

This book is such an apology and a warning: *Hyper-Calvinism & the Call of the Gospel.*

Chapter 1
Hyper-Calvinism

In most cases the charge "hyper-Calvinism" is nothing but a deceptive attack upon Calvinism itself. Someone hates Calvinism or the uncompromising, consistent defense of Calvinism. Yet he hesitates to attack Calvinism openly and forthrightly. Therefore he disguises his attack as an attack on "hyper-Calvinism" and "hyper-Calvinists."

An outstanding and clear example of this cowardly, deceitful method of attacking Calvinism is the attack on Calvinism by the self-styled evangelist John R. Rice in two books, *Some Serious Popular False Doctrines* and *Predestined for Hell? No!* Chapter 7 of the former is entitled "Hyper-Calvinism — A False Doctrine," and the cover of the latter explains that the author is busy "correcting the errors of Hyper-Calvinism." Under pretense of opposing hyper-Calvinism, Rice fights the truth that men are saved by God's sovereign grace alone and propounds the ancient heresy that man saves himself by the exercise of his free-will.

This is obvious in the scurrilous little book *Predestined for Hell? No!*[1] The author's tactics are the despicable tactics that the Arminians have always used against the Reformed faith. As the title indicates, the attack on election and salvation by sovereign grace alone is launched specifically against the doctrine of reprobation. The crafty Arminians are aware that men have more natural antipathy to reprobation than to any other

---

1. John R. Rice, *Predestined for Hell? No!* (Murfreesboro, Tennessee: Sword of the Lord Foundation, 1958).

doctrine and feel that they can put the Reformed faith in a bad light from the outset if they succeed in making reprobation the first and main subject of debate. This was exactly what Episcopius and the Arminian party tried to do at Dordt when, having failed in their political maneuverings, they proposed to the Synod that the Synod first take up the doctrine of reprobation.[2]

Then the author caricatures reprobation. On the cover of his book is this picture: a disconsolate, unwilling man is forced into the livid flames of hell at the point of a sword tyrannically wielded by the arm of God. Already on the third page of the book, Calvinists are epitomized as people who teach that "there are babes in Hell not a span long."

The contents of the book are an open, all-out assault upon the first four of the well-known five points of Calvinism, a rejection of total depravity, unconditional election, limited atonement, and irresistible grace.[3]

---

2. The Synod wisely and justly refused to follow this order. It began with election and salvation by God's free and sovereign grace. The answer to the question "Are some men sovereignly and eternally ordained by God to hell?" is "yes." But this is not primary. God's election of His church in Jesus Christ is primary. Nor is reprobation the issue between the Reformed and the Arminians. Gracious salvation founded on election is the issue. Today also, we defenders of gracious salvation must not allow the Arminians to set the agenda or to determine what shall be emphasized as primary and central.

3. Rice claims to believe the fifth point of Calvinism, the perseverance of saints, which he calls "eternal security." This is an insignificant oddity of some in the Arminian camp. Someone has wittily characterized this position of some Arminians as the teaching that "you can get in by yourself (i.e., into salvation), but you can't get out." In reality, there is a basic difference between Rice's teaching of eternal security and the Reformed doctrine of perseverance. For Rice and his ilk, eternal security is the certainty that

What it is that Rice hates with all his heart becomes plain when he quotes the man who is for Rice the quintessential hyper-Calvinist, Herman Hoeksema. To illustrate hyper-Calvinism, Rice quotes from Hoeksema's *Whosoever Will.*[4] What does Hoeksema write in the offensive paragraph? That God is a tyrant Who shuts His ears to the pleas of poor sinners to be saved and thrusts them, willy-nilly, into hell? Nothing of the sort. Rather, Hoeksema proclaims these truths: "(salvation) is absolutely divine. Man ... cannot possibly cooperate with God in his own salvation.... The sinner is of himself neither capable nor willing to receive that salvation.... But God ordained, and prepared this salvation with absolutely sovereign freedom for His own, His chosen ones alone, and upon them He bestows it...." This is all: the total depravity of man by nature; salvation by free, sovereign grace alone; God's gracious election of some men unto salvation. This, says Rice, is the height of hyper-Calvinism. But in reality, it is simply Calvinism, the historic Reformed faith.

There is no need to refute Rice's arguments against Calvinism nor to expose his defense of Arminianism from Scripture, although a lover of the Reformed faith is sorely tempted to do this in order to lay bare the utter poverty of modern Arminianism. Rice blunders around in the Bible, as Luther said of Erasmus, the way a pig roots about in a sack of feed.

It serves our purpose to stress two things regarding

---

everyone who makes a cheap decision for Christ will go to heaven, no matter how he lives after he has made the decision. The Reformed doctrine of perseverance is the truth that God preserves the regenerated elect through sanctification of life (cf. the Canons of Dordt, V).

4.   Rice, *Predestined,* p. 11; cf. also pp. 95ff.

the war-cry "hyper-Calvinism" that become plain from such works as those of John Rice.

First, the charge "hyper-Calvinism" masks an attack on *Calvinism*. Rice is an Arminian and a Pelagian. He admits to holding that every man's salvation depends on the choice of his own free will. This is Arminianism. He also maintains that men only *potentially* died in Adam and that the natural man who has nothing more than the testimony of God in creation may be saved by this natural light. This is sheer Pelagianism. Rice is guilty of the one, great, "serious, popular false doctrine": man saves himself by his own willing and running. As such, he is an inveterate foe of Calvinism which maintains the true doctrine: man's salvation is of God Who shows mercy (Rom. 9:16).

The attack on Calvinism by means of the charge "hyper-Calvinism" is another of the calumnies heaped upon the Reformed faith, as the Conclusion of the Canons of Dordt puts it. It is reproach for Christ's sake that Reformed people must suffer in this life. But we do, with the Conclusion of the Canons, warn the calumniators "to consider the terrible judgment of God which awaits them," and we do urge as many as piously call upon the name of Jesus not to judge our faith on the basis of the accusations of our enemies. In light of the fact that foes of the Reformed faith have always misrepresented that faith, men today ought at least to consider that the charge "hyper-Calvinists" might be a cheap shot at a thorough-going, consistent Calvinism.

Second, it is significant that the heart of Rice's opposition to Calvinism is his insistence that the doctrines of Calvinism make preaching, particularly the call of the gospel, impossible. In Rice's terminology, Calvinism destroys "soul-winning." He writes: "This doctrine (i.e., Calvinism — DJE) insists that we need not urge a

man to turn to Christ. He cannot turn until God forces
him to do so. If God has planned for him to be eternally
lost, he will not be turned to God. If God has planned
for him to be saved, then 'irresistible grace,' the hyper-
Calvinist says, will force him to be saved." In the
chapter entitled "The Harm Done by Hyper-Calvinism
Heresy," the first two alleged evil consequences of
Calvinism are: "I. Hyper-Calvinists Actually Hinder
and Oppose Gospel Preaching and Soul Winning" and
"II. Hyper-Calvinism is Either Indifferent to or Opposed to Foreign Missions."[5]

This was the charge laid against the Reformed faith
by the Arminians at the time of the Synod of Dordt. The
Arminians argued that election, limited atonement, and
sovereign grace ruled out the serious call of the gospel
to all who hear the preaching. In the Canons the
Reformed churches proved that the charge was false
and that the lively preaching, including the serious call
to repentance and faith, retains its full rights within the
framework of the doctrines of Calvinism. The Reformed faith does full justice to preaching, including the
call of the gospel, *while holding wholeheartedly and without
qualifications to predestination, limited atonement, and irresistible grace.* Its response to the monotonous Arminian
allegation that it has no place for the call of the gospel is
never that it hedges on or compromises predestination
and sovereign grace.

This is forgotten by many Calvinists today to the
peril of the faith that they profess to love. To the charge
that the Reformed faith cannot in the preaching call all
who hear to repent and believe, they respond by compromising the essential doctrines of Calvinism. By

5. Ibid.

adopting the theory of the well-meant offer of the gospel, these churches begin saying "yes and no" to the great Calvinistic doctrines of grace: "Yes, God loved and chose only some men, but, no, He also loves and desires to save everybody"; "Yes, God's grace in the preaching is irresistible, but, no, God's grace for some in the preaching fails to save them"; "Yes, Christ of the cross is only for the elect, but, no, He is also for the reprobate." This is the theology of the offer. This is not the way to make place in the Reformed system for the serious call of the gospel to all who hear. This is not the way to safeguard the lively preaching. It is the way to surrender the Reformed faith. It is the way to lose the gospel of grace itself.

If the charge "hyper-Calvinism" is usually a disguised attack on Calvinism itself, the question arises whether there has ever been, or is now, a theology that may correctly be called hyper-Calvinism. Or is the charge nothing but a theological bugbear?

We will not concern ourselves with the terms themselves, whether "Calvinism" is a good name for the Reformed faith and whether "hyper-Calvinism" is an accurate description of a theology that has fundamentally perverted genuine Calvinism. We are concerned only with the question whether some who professed Calvinism have drawn unbiblical and unwarranted inferences from the doctrines of Calvinism so that their doctrine and practice went "beyond Calvinism" and deserved to be called hyper-Calvinism.

The answer to this question is that there has been a teaching and corresponding practice that can rightly be called hyper-Calvinism and that could give occasion to some today (mistakenly) to regard the denial of the well-meant offer of the gospel by the Protestant Reformed Churches as hyper-Calvinism. It is important, however, to be clear as to what it is that takes a theology beyond the pale of true Calvinism into the realm of hyper-Calvinism.

Contrary to the thinking of some, the doctrine of supralapsarianism does not make one a hyper-Calvinist. There has always been room in the Reformed faith for supralapsarianism.[6] Although the Reformed confessions are infralapsarian, the Canons of Dordt deliberately so over against the strong plea of Gomarus for supralapsarianism, they do not condemn supralapsarianism as unreformed or hyper-Calvinistic.

Nor is one a hyper-Calvinist because he holds the doctrines of eternal justification and immediate regeneration. Sound Reformed theologians have both denied and affirmed these teachings.

Neither is it the case that hyper-Calvinism is a matter of a strong emphasis on God's eternal counsel and God's sovereignty in salvation. No true Calvinist ever lacked this strong emphasis.

But hyper-Calvinism is the denial that God in the preaching of the gospel calls everyone who hears the preaching to repent and believe. It is the denial that the

---

6. Such Calvinists as Theodore Beza, Abraham Kuyper, and Herman Hoeksema were supralapsarians. The issue of infralapsarianism vs. supralapsarianism concerns the order of God's decrees. The basic question at issue is this: does the decree of predestination *precede* or *follow* the decree of man's fall in the eternal counsel of God? Supralapsarianism holds that the decree of predestination is before (Latin: *supra*) the decree of the fall (Latin: *lapsus*); infralapsarianism holds that the decree of predestination follows upon (Latin: *infra*) the decree of the fall. Both supralapsarianism and infralapsarianism confess that God decreed the fall of man and that the decree of predestination is an eternal decree. They are one in setting forth predestination as a sovereign, unconditional, eternal, double decree of God.

church should call everyone in the preaching. It is the denial that the unregenerated have a duty to repent and believe. It manifests itself in the practice of the preacher's addressing the call of the gospel, "repent and believe on Christ crucified," only to those in his audience who show signs of regeneration and, thereby, of election, namely, some conviction of sin and some interest in salvation.

This error actually appeared in the history of Calvinism in England.[7] It was the position of several Congregational and Baptist ministers, including Joseph Hussey (1660-1726), Lewis Wayman (died 1764), John Brine (1703-1765), and the well-known John Gill (born 1697). Wayman, Brine, and Gill were involved in a theological controversy known as "the Modern Question." "The Modern Question" was: "Whether saving faith in Christ is a duty required by the moral law of all those who live under the Gospel revelation?" Basically, the question was whether the reprobate unbeliever is required by God in the preaching to believe in Christ. Wayman, Brine, and Gill denied this. Since many New Testament passages plainly teach that Christ and the apostles did in fact command everyone in their audience to repent

---

7. For this history, but not for the analysis of it, I am largely dependent on Peter Toon's *The Emergence of Hyper-Calvinism in English Nonconformity 1689-1765* (London: The Olive Tree, 1967). Cf. also Andrew Fuller, *The Complete Works of the Rev. Andrew Fuller* (London: G. and J. Dyer, Paternoster Row, 1845), especially "The Gospel Worthy of All Acceptation, or the Duty of Sinners to Believe in Jesus Christ." Fuller opposes the hyper-Calvinism of Brine, although he regards Hussey and Gill as in agreement with Brine. Even though Fuller's expressions are not always soundly Reformed, it is clear from his writings that his opponents denied that faith is the duty of the ungodly and, therefore, that the call of the gospel comes to them.

and believe, the reprobate as well as the elect, these men resorted to a distinction between legal and evangelical repentance and between common and saving faith. "Legal repentance" and "common faith," according to this distinction, are virtually synonymous with the demand of the law, which God makes of everyone; "evangelical repentance" and "saving faith," then, make up the real gospel call, which God gives only to the regenerated elect. This artificial and impossible distinction only serves to make plain that these men denied that God calls everyone who hears the preaching to repent of his sins and to believe on the Christ presented in the gospel and that it is the duty of every man who comes under the preaching to repent and believe. But these men called their position "the denial of the offers of grace," and this is what many think of when they hear that a church denies the offer of the gospel.

The Gospel Standard (Baptist) Churches in England continue to maintain this hyper-Calvinism as several articles of their confession show:

> XXVI. We deny duty faith and duty repentance — these terms signifying that it is every man's duty spiritually and savingly to repent and believe (Gen. 6:5; 8:21; Matt. 15:19; Jer. 17:9; John 6:44, 65). We deny also that there is any capability in man by nature to any spiritual good whatever. So that we reject the doctrine that men in a state of nature should be exhorted to believe in or turn to God (John 12:39, 40; Eph. 2:8; Rom. 8:7, 8; I Cor. 4:7).
>
> XXXIII. Therefore, that for ministers in the present day to address unconverted persons, or indiscriminately all in a mixed congregation, calling upon them savingly to repent, believe, and receive Christ, or perform

18

Hyper-Calvinism

any other acts dependent upon the new creative power of the Holy Ghost, is, on the one hand, to imply creature power, and, on the other, to deny the doctrine of special redemption.

XXXIV. We believe that any such expressions as convey to the hearers the belief that they possess a certain power to flee to the Saviour, to close in with Christ, to receive Christ, while in an unregenerate state, so that unless they do thus close with Christ, etc., they shall perish, are untrue, and must, therefore, be rejected. And we further believe that we have no scripture warrant to take the exhortations in the Old Testament intended for the Jews in national covenant with God, and apply them in a spiritual and saving sense to unregenerated men.[8]

There are also Baptist churches in the United States which vehemently oppose "the offer of the gospel" in the name of Calvinism, but which are actually opposed to calling anyone to believe on Christ except the regenerated elect.

It seems that men fell into this error in reaction to the rising Arminianism of their time. Gill, e.g., was a contemporary of the notorious, admitted Arminian John Wesley. It may even be the case that the practice of referring to the call of the gospel as "the offer" contributed to the error of the English hyper-Calvinists. At issue, in reality, was that which Reformed theology speaks of as "the external call of the gospel." But both

8. *Articles of Faith of the Gospel Standard Aid and Poor Relief Societies* (Leicester, England: Oldham & Manton Ltd., n.d.), pp. 14, 16, 17.

parties in the controversy referred to this call as "the offer of the gospel."[9] Since the term "offer" has the Arminian flavor, it is not surprising that the would-be defenders of Calvinism rejected the offer, especially since the Arminian conception of the offer was rampant at that time. The trouble was that in throwing out the bath-water, they threw out the baby, that is, the external call to all who hear the gospel, reprobate and elect alike.

Those who repudiated the external call of the gospel to all who hear certainly supposed that they were defending Calvinism. This is why their error may be called hyper-Calvinism. This is plain especially in Article 33 of the confessional articles of the Gospel Standard Churches. It argues that a call to an unconverted person to repent and believe would imply "creature power," that is, the ability of that unconverted person to do what he was called to do. In other words, the call to the unconverted would imply free will and would be a denial of total depravity. Also, such a call would be a denial of "the doctrine of special redemption," that is, the doctrine of limited atonement. The argument is that if all are called to believe in Christ, Christ must have died for all and must desire to be the Savior of all. But since Christ died only for the elect, only the elect are to be called in the preaching.

Although put forth as true Calvinism, the teaching that denies the call of the gospel to all who hear the preaching is not Reformed, biblical doctrine. It is indeed

---

9.   Hussey's book was entitled *God's Operations of Grace but No Offers of His Grace*. This book has been published in an abridged edition by Primitive Publications, Elon College, North Carolina. Andrew Fuller, criticizing the hyper-Calvinism of Hussey and the others, asserted "the free offer of salvation to sinners."

true that God calls only the predestinated, or elect, with the effectual, saving call. Them and them only, He calls by drawing them efficaciously to Himself by a sovereign work of the Holy Spirit in their hearts even as He says "Come!" in the preaching of the gospel. This is the teaching of Romans 8:30: "Moreover whom he did predestinate, them he also called...." But there is also a sense, according to Scripture, in which He calls those who are not elect in the preaching of the gospel. Matthew 22:14 teaches this: "For many are called, but few are chosen." More people than the elect are called by God. As is plain from the parable that precedes, the parable of the king's wedding feast, the reference is to the call that God makes through His church and her preachers when He commands all who hear the gospel to repent of their sins and believe on Jesus Christ. God calls men to come to the feast of salvation prepared through Jesus' death and resurrection. The response of many to this call is that they reject it. By doing so, they bring down upon themselves the wrathful judgment of God, terrible exactly because it is the punishment for rejecting the call of the gospel. Theirs is the sin of sins: despising Christ presented to them in the gospel and rejecting God's call to believe on Him.

That the call to repent is not restricted to the regenerated, or "the sensible sinner," but goes out to everyone who hears the preaching is taught in Acts 17:30: "(God) now commandeth all men everywhere to repent." This was the practice of the apostles. Having proclaimed Christ to their audience, they called everyone to repent of his sins and to believe on Christ (see Acts 3:19; 8:22; 13:38-41; 20:21). This was the ministry of John the Baptist. He "came ... preaching ... and saying, Repent ye." He called also the Pharisees and Sadducees, "(a) generation of vipers," to "bring forth therefore fruits meet for repentance" (Matt. 3:1-12). Such was the nature of the preaching of Jesus Himself: "Jesus came into Galilee, preaching the gospel of the kingdom of God, And saying, The time is fulfilled, and the kingdom of God is at hand; repent ye, and believe the gospel" (Mark 1:14, 15).

What the Reformed faith, genuine Calvinism, confesses concerning the call of the gospel is set forth plainly in the Reformed creed, the Canons of Dordt. The promise that believers have eternal life and the command to repent and believe must be proclaimed "to all nations, and to all persons promiscuously and without distinction, to whom God out of his good pleasure sends the gospel" (II/5). God Himself "unfeignedly," that is, seriously, calls everyone who hears the gospel. He does this through the gospel itself. As He calls, He "most earnestly and truly" declares that it is "acceptable" to Him that "all who are called, should come unto Him" (III, IV/8). One result of this serious call of the gospel is that many "refuse to come, and be converted." This is not the gospel's fault, nor Christ's fault, nor God's fault, but it is their own fault, for they wickedly reject the word of life (III, IV/9). However, there is also the result that some obey the call of the gospel and are converted. This is not due to free will or any ability in them "whereby one distinguishes himself above others," but it is due to the sovereign grace of God alone. The reason why some come to Christ is that God efficaciously draws them by His Spirit. And He draws them, in distinction from others, because He has eternally elected them, whereas He eternally reprobated the others (III, IV/10; cf. also I/6).

The Canons powerfully refute the Arminian charge that the doctrines of predestination, limited atonement, total depravity, irresistible grace, and the perseverance of saints hinder, if they do not altogether nullify, the lively preaching, especially the gospel call. What is so striking is the Canons' refusal to react to the Arminian heresy by denying the call of the gospel to everyone, or even by becoming timid and hesitant concerning this call. They show that the Reformed faith will not allow Arminianism to drive it into the opposite error of hyper-Calvinism.

This, however, was exactly what happened to those who denied the call of the gospel to all who hear the preaching. Those who denied the external call of the gospel out of the fear that this compromised Calvinism were mistaken on two counts. First, they erred in supposing that the call or command to unregenerated unbelievers would imply the ability of the unregenerated to do what God required, namely, repent and believe. They argued that for God or for the church to call everybody to believe on Christ would imply the false doctrine of free will. That this was the error of the hyper-Calvinists is evident from Article 33 of the confessional articles of the Gospel Standard Churches: "to address unconverted persons ... calling upon them to savingly repent, believe and receive Christ ... is ... to imply creature power...." Oddly enough, this is the very same mistake that the Pelagians and Arminians have always made: to suppose that the exhortations and demands of the Scriptures imply the ability of man to fulfill the demands. The Pelagians and Arminians have always argued that, since God commands men to believe, men must have the ability to believe. The hyper-Calvinist, on the other hand, agreeing that the call to believe would imply free will, denies the call. The error of both is their failure to see that the call of God to sinners in no way presupposes the ability of sinners to heed the call.

Luther exposed the error of the notion that a command of God implies a corresponding ability in man in his controversy with the Pelagian Erasmus over the bondage of the will. Responding to Erasmus' defense of a free will on the ground that God calls men to choose, turn, and repent, Luther wrote:

> ...by the words of the law man is admonished and taught, not what he can do, but what he ought to do.
> How is it that you theologians are twice as stupid as schoolboys, in that as soon as you get hold of a single imperative verb you infer an indicative meaning, as though the moment a thing is commanded it is done, or can be done?
> The passages of Scripture which you cite are imperative; and they prove and establish nothing about the ability of man, but only lay down what is and is not to be done.[10]

Question 9 of the Heidelberg Catechism teaches, as regards the demand of perfect obedience that God makes in His law, that God does exactly require of men that which they are incapable of doing: "Doth not God then do injustice to man, by requiring from him in His law, that which he cannot perform? Answer — Not at all; for God made man capable of performing it; but man, by the instigation of the devil, and his own wilful disobedience, deprived himself and all his posterity of those divine gifts." Although the Catechism is speaking here of God's demand on men in the law, the principle holds good for the command to repent and believe

10. Martin Luther, *The Bondage of the Will*, tr. J.I. Packer and O.R. Johnston (London: James Clarke & Co., Ltd. 1957), pp. 151ff.

which God gives to the unregenerated in the gospel. The call to believe does not imply, nor is it based on, the free will of the sinner. Rather, it sets forth man's duty and shows man what it is that pleases God.

The second error of the hyper-Calvinistic denial of the call of the gospel was the fear that a call of the gospel to the unregenerated wicked would jeopardize the doctrines of election and limited atonement. This is evident in Article 33 of the Gospel Standard Churches, quoted above, which continues: "... and ... to deny the doctrine of special redemption." This would indeed be true if the call to the reprobate expressed God's love for him and manifested a desire of God to save him. But such is not the case. When God sends the gospel forth into all the world, presenting Christ crucified to all who hear the preaching and calling all who hear to repent of their sins and believe on that Christ, His purpose is to save the elect and the elect only. The love that sends forth the gospel, like the love that sent forth Christ in the fullness of time, is the love of God for the elect church. This love is sovereign love. As the call to repent and believe goes out, God the Holy Spirit *works that repentance and faith in the hearts of the elect in the audience.* He gives us what He calls for, and He gives it by the calling. "Come!" He says, and that sovereignly gracious call draws us irresistibly to Christ.

This is the confidence of every preacher when he calls men to repent and believe: God will make it effective in the elect. With regard to the others in the audience, the call comes to them also, *seriously.* But the call does not express God's love for them, nor does it imply that Jesus died for them. By the call, God confronts them with their duty and shows them what will be pleasing to Him. But His purpose with the call to them is not a saving purpose. On the contrary, it is His purpose to render them inexcusable and to harden them (Rom. 9:18; see also Matt. 11:25-27).

There is always a twofold outcome of the preaching of the gospel, including the serious call of the gospel to all who hear. This outcome occurs according to the sovereign purpose of God *with this preaching and call:* "Now thanks be unto God, which always causeth us to triumph in Christ, and maketh manifest the savour of his knowledge by us in every place. For we are unto God a sweet savour of Christ, in them that are saved, and in them that perish: To the one we are the savour of death unto death; and to the other the savour of life unto life. And who is sufficient for these things?" (II Cor. 2:14-16).

The practical effects of the hyper-Calvinistic denial of the call of the gospel to all and sundry and of the attempt to limit it to the reborn elect are disastrous. Basically, the effect is nothing less than the loss of the lively preaching of the gospel, first in the sphere of missions, and then, inevitably, within the church herself. The classic example is the well-known response of J.C. Ryland, close friend of John Gill, to William Carey's plea for mission societies to preach the gospel in India: "Sit down, young man. When God pleases to convert the heathen He will do it without your aid and mine." Although old Ryland may have been concerned to guard against the corruption of missions by Arminianism, his notion that God's sovereignty in salvation makes preaching on the mission field unnecessary was false. Applied consistently, this notion would rule out not only preaching to the heathen but also preaching to the saints. The biblical rejoinder and the Reformed confession is: the sovereign God is pleased to save His people through the preaching of the gospel.

To strip the call from the preaching is to do violence to the gospel itself. The call to believe is not an appendage of the gospel, to be tacked on awkwardly at the end like the proverbial tail on the donkey. It is an inherent part of the gospel itself. Whenever and wherever the gospel is preached, the call to repent and believe is sounded to all who hear, whether explicitly or implicitly. Usually the apostles made the call explicit: "Repent! Believe!" Sometimes the call was implied, e.g., in the sermon at Pisidian Antioch recorded in Acts 13. Paul did not explicitly say, "Believe." But his statement in verse 39 that justification comes only by faith in Christ, not from the law, and his warning in verses 40 and 41 against refusing to believe sound the call loudly and clearly: "Believe on this crucified and risen Christ!" The message proclaimed in the gospel is not something that may ever merely be received for information, nor does it ever leave anyone with the impression that God is satisfied with that. The message of the gospel is the message of God's Son in our flesh, crucified and risen for the forgiveness of sins and eternal life. The gospel must be believed, and the Christ presented in the gospel must be believed on—*today*. Nothing else will do. Therefore, the gospel *calls* those who hear the good news.

Also, the attempt to limit the call to the regenerated is a hopeless task. It sets before any minister an impossible task. Before he may call a sinner to repent and believe, he must determine that the sinner is born again. Even if a person reveals some sorrow for sin, he ought to determine whether the sorrow is godly sorrow or the sorrow of the world. The result will be that a man, fearful of compromising Calvinism by calling an unregenerate, will call almost no one. This is to reverse God's operations. For the sake of the elect, God has the church call all who hear the preaching; lest it call a reprobate, hyper-Calvinism tends to call no one.

Condemnation of hyper-Calvinism, however, does

not touch the Protestant Reformed rejection of the well-meant gospel offer. Between the serious call to all who hear the gospel and the well-meant offer of the gospel, there is a vast gulf fixed, the gulf that separates the historic Reformed faith from Arminianism.

Chapter 2
The Well-Meant Offer of the Gospel

Throughout their history up to the present day, the Protestant Reformed Churches have been misrepresented as hyper-Calvinists because of their denial of the well-meant offer of the gospel. This has been done by charging that they preach only to the elect, by charging that they refuse to call everyone to Christ, by charging that they do not believe in missions, and by outrightly referring to them as hyper-Calvinists. In various ways, men have represented these churches' opposition to the well-meant offer of the gospel as a denial of the serious call of the gospel to all who hear the preaching and a weakening of the church's calling to preach the gospel to every creature, commanding all who come under the preaching to repent and believe. This is total, and usually inexcusable, misrepresentation.

A.C. DeJong did this in his book *The Well-Meant Gospel Offer: The Views of H. Hoeksema and K. Schilder,*[1] a book that has framed the opinion that many have of the Protestant Reformed Churches' denial of the well-meant offer. The book is DeJong's doctoral thesis for G.C. Berkouwer. Berkouwer has given the book and its representation of Hoeksema's denial of the offer wide circulation by his repeated reference to it in his dogmat-

---

1.   A.C. DeJong, *The Well-Meant Gospel Offer: The Views of H. Hoeksema and K. Schilder* (Franeker: T. Wever, 1954).

ics as an authoritative, reliable analysis of Hoeksema's
teaching on the offer and preaching.[2]

One wonders whether a man like M.J. Arntzen,
fighting the war for the Reformed faith in the Netherlands, has not uncritically accepted DeJong's distorted
presentation of Hoeksema's position. In his little book
De Crisis in de Gereformeerde Kerken, Arntzen contends
earnestly for the doctrine of election since this is one of
the fundamental truths presently being undermined in
the Reformed Churches in the Netherlands, largely
through the influence of Berkouwer. In the course of his
defense of election, Arntzen necessarily confronts "the
well-meant offer of grace." This brings up Hoeksema's
denial of the offer. Arntzen criticizes Hoeksema for this
denial. He speaks of "the error of Hoeksema." He
thinks that Hoeksema "does not remain free from speculation." Hoeksema's conceptions are "very extreme."
Having surveyed the debate over the offer, Arntzen
claims that he does "not belong to the opponents of such
an offer."

But apparently Arntzen knows Hoeksema's position, as well as the controversy over the offer, only
through the book of A.C. DeJong. Even then, Arntzen
is not at all satisfied either with DeJong's doctrine of the
well-meant offer or with DeJong's condemnation of
Hoeksema. He sees that DeJong is guilty of the "opposite error" of denying that there is any difference in
God's call to men according to God's good pleasure.
According to DeJong, God calls all men in the same,
powerful way, thus implying that grace is resistible and
that regeneration can be annulled.

---

2. See Berkouwer, *Divine Election*, pp. 221-228. Reference to it
is found also in Berkouwer's *A Half Century of Theology*, trans.
and ed. Lewis B. Smedes (Grand Rapids: Wm. B. Eerdmans
Publishing Co., 1977), p. 99.

When he comes to confess his own belief of the offer, Arntzen uses words to which Hoeksema could, and would, say "amen," but which do not at all express the well-meant offer of the gospel: "that God is serious *(het ernstig meent)* over against every one who is called, and that it is acceptable to God, to use the language of the Canons, that those who are called come to Him."

In spite of his claims to the contrary, Arntzen simply cannot rest easy with the offer of grace, especially not in view of the use of the offer to make war on divine predestination and limited atonement: "The disproportionately strong emphasis on the universal offer of grace must inevitably lead to a preaching of universal atonement." He struggles with the relationship between election and the offer: "We want to express the hope that there would appear once a ... study of election and of the universal offer of grace which does not allow itself to be influenced by all kinds of modern theological and philosophical presuppositions, but which is purely Biblical."[3]

What Arntzen does not seem to see is that men illegitimately identify the serious call of the Canons with the well-meant offer in order, then, with this club to beat to death the Reformed doctrine of predestination. Defense of the doctrine of election demands that the well-meant offer be condemned. But condemnation of the offer is *not* rejection of the serious call of the gospel to all who hear. This is the impression, however, that DeJong left in his *The Well-Meant Gospel Offer.*

DeJong criticized Hoeksema's denial of the offer as a virtual destruction of lively gospel preaching. He

---

3. M.J. Arntzen, *De Crisis in de Gereformeerde Kerken* (Amsterdam: Buijten & Schipperheijn, 1965), pp. 43-64. The translation of the Dutch is mine.

suggested that Hoeksema's rejection of the offer means that Hoeksema cannot, indeed does not want to, preach to all and that Hoeksema cannot call everyone who hears the preaching to believe on Christ. For Hoeksema, preaching becomes "the communication of a certain group of logically interrelated doctrines.... There is in Hoeksema's theology a subtle mutation of preaching into a report of an objective and fixed set of circumstances." Hoeksema merely "admits that all sinners are called to repent and believe." But his denial of the offer really makes this impossible: he can only call men "to a decision for or against a set of truths...." Because he denies the offer, Hoeksema is guilty of "restricting the proclamation of the good news that whosoever believeth on Christ shall not perish but have eternal life. He cannot personally address the good news." DeJong speaks of Hoeksema's "depreciation of genuine responsibility and real decision."[4] In short, Hoeksema is a hyper-Calvinist, unwilling to preach the good news promiscuously and unable to call all sinners, in all seriousness, to repentance and faith.

We must refrain from taking up DeJong's amazing assertion that preaching is not "in the first moment the communication of a certain group of ... doctrines" and that preaching is not "in the first instance an explication of an objective set of circumstances (or) a communication of a certain truth," but that preaching is "in the first moment" and "in the first instance" a "summons to share in Christ's victory over sin."[5] "In the first instance," preaching is exactly the communication of doctrine and truth, that is, the announcement of that which God has done and will do in Jesus Christ. It is the

4.   A.C. DeJong, *Well-Meant Gospel Offer*, pp. 110, 111, 123, 177.
5.   Ibid., pp. 110, 111.

official declaration of *news*, the good news of God's gracious salvation. It is the "explication of an objective set of circumstances": "Christ died for our sins according to the scriptures ... and he rose again the third day..." (I Cor. 15:3, 4). Good, apostolic gospel-preaching is, in addition, a declaration of "all the counsel of God" (Acts 20:27). Then, and only then, it is also a "testifying ... repentance toward God, and faith toward our Lord Jesus Christ" (Acts 20:21).

To construe preaching as "in the first moment" in the imperative mood (telling man what he must do) and not in the indicative mood (telling man what God has done and promises to do) is to produce the monstrosity that passes for gospel-preaching today: a few minutes about Jesus followed by a twenty minute altar call.[6] But we let this go. Our concern is only to show that Hoeksema's denial of the offer had nothing to do with any hesitancy on Hoeksema's part to give a summons to all who come under the preaching to believe on Christ and that his denial of the offer implies no restriction of full, lively gospel-preaching.

---

6. How serious a matter this is, J. Gresham Machen brought out in his *Christianity and Liberalism:* "From the beginning, the Christian gospel, as indeed the name 'gospel' or 'good news' implies, consisted in an account of something that had happened. And from the beginning, the meaning of the happening was set forth; and when the meaning of the happening was set forth then there was Christian doctrine.... It is perfectly clear, then, that the first Christian missionaries did not simply come forward with an exhortation...." Again, "Here is found the most fundamental difference between liberalism and Christianity — liberalism is altogether in the imperative mood, while Christianity begins with a triumphant indicative; liberalism appeals to man's will, while Christianity announces, first, a gracious act of God" (Grand Rapids: Wm. B. Eerdmans Publishing Co., 1923), pp. 27, 47.

What it is that the Protestant Reformed Churches object to in the well-meant offer of the gospel, what the issue really is in their denial of the offer, is made crystal clear in Herman Hoeksema's book, *Een Kracht Gods Tot Zaligheid of Genade Geen Aanbod (A Power of God unto Salvation, or Grace No Offer).* Already in the earliest history of the Protestant Reformed Churches, men tried to leave the impression that the issue was the failure of the Protestant Reformed Churches to do justice to the call of the gospel to everyone who hears the preaching. Hoeksema insisted that this was misrepresentation and that the issue was something quite different.

A certain Rev. Keegstra had written that Hoeksema's denial of the well-meant offer of the gospel as adopted by the Christian Reformed Church in 1924 was really a denial that the gospel must be preached to everyone and a denial that God seriously calls everyone who hears the preaching to repent and believe. Against Keegstra, Hoeksema wrote that the issue involved in denying the offer had nothing to do with the question whether the gospel should be preached to everyone:

> Our difference does not at all have to do with the question, whether the gospel, according to the will of God, must also be preached to all who are in our audience, reprobate as well as elect. This is taken for granted on both sides. Note well, (the issue) is not whether the gospel must be proclaimed by the preacher to all men who sit in his audience without distinction. Every Reformed man believes this.[7]

---

7.   Hoeksema, *Een Kracht Gods,* pp. 20, 27.

Nor is this the issue, that the Protestant Reformed Churches dislike to *call* everyone who hears the preaching:

> We have nothing against a universal *demand* of faith and conversion. About this there is no dispute.... That the demand of conversion and faith applies to all, even though all cannot fulfill it and even though it is only almighty grace that enables one to fulfill it, we readily grant.[8]

Hoeksema expresses agreement with Calvin who taught "that through the ministry of the gospel by men, many are called in the external sense of the word; called to faith and conversion; called to the salvation in Christ; that many come under the promise: whoever believes has eternal life. But this is something entirely different from confessing that God now well-meaningly offers His salvation in Christ to all who hear the Word."[9]

Almost impatiently, Hoeksema rejected the misrepresentation of his stand against the offer:

> Let us keep this point firmly in mind. The question is not what God demands. The question is also not whether God wills that the gospel shall be preached to all without distinction to whom He sends it according to His good pleasure. No, the question is simply this: is that gospel according to its content a well-meaning and common offer on God's part?... Rev. Keegstra, please, there is between us no difference over the fact that many who

---

8. Ibid., p. 30.
9. Ibid., p. 63.

are called by the gospel perish in their unbelief!
Nor is there any question between us about
the equally firm fact that the guilt of such
unbelief does not lie in any lack in Christ, but
in themselves.[10]

Why did Hoeksema refuse to subscribe to the doctrine of the well-meant offer of the gospel even though
the price he paid was expulsion from the Christian
Reformed Church? Why do the Protestant Reformed
Churches repudiate the offer today?

Hoeksema opposed the doctrine of the well-meant
offer of the gospel that was taught by the Christian
Reformed Church in the first point of common grace of
1924. The teaching of that first point is that God has a
"favorable attitude ... towards humanity in general and
not only towards the elect," that there is "a certain favor
or grace of God which He shows to His creatures in
general," and that "the general offer of the gospel" is an
expression of that favor or grace of God to all men. With
reference to this first point of common grace and its
doctrine of the offer, Hoeksema wrote:

> What is the real point of the first point (het
> puntje van dit eerste punt)? Only this, that the
> offer of the gospel is common? No, but that
> this offer of the gospel *is common grace*
> (emphasis his — DJE). The preaching of the
> gospel, so the Synod of 1924 has taught, is
> God's grace, not only for the elect, but also for
> the reprobate, not only for those who are
> saved by it, but also for those who perish
> under it. That is the point. The preaching of
> the gospel is *grace for all*.[11]

10. Ibid., pp. 68, 105.
11. Ibid., pp. 16, 17.

The well-meant offer teaches that God goes out in the preaching to many sinners in love and grace, desiring to save them and trying to save them, but failing to save them. Concerning such a view Hoeksema wrote:

> I find this in one word, terrible. For to me it is nothing less than a direct denial of the almighty grace of the Savior, a denial of the sovereign grace of God; an enthronement of the will of man.[12]

The issue at stake in the doctrine of the offer is nothing less than the truth of sovereign grace: "The standpoint of 1924 is Arminian. That the preaching of the gospel is common grace — this is the Arminian conception."[13] In opposition to the well-meant offer, Hoeksema held, not that there is no call to all who hear the gospel but that "the preaching of the gospel is grace *only* for the elect, and that it is not and can never be anything else for the reprobate than a judgment and a savor of death to death." This is the issue: this is "our difference with the Christian Reformed Church"[14]

The well-meant offer teaches that God's grace is universal. The Protestant Reformed Churches maintain that God's grace is particular, specifically now in the preaching of the gospel. The truth that God's grace is particular is essential for a confession of the *sovereignty* of grace. If God's grace in the preaching is for everybody, it is not sovereign grace. And the truth that God's grace in the preaching of the gospel is particular, sovereign grace is the very heart of the Reformed faith:

---

12. Ibid., p. 45.
13. Ibid., p. 17.
14. Ibid., p. 17.

> For him who loves the Reformed faith, the
> confession that God's grace is particular is of
> the very highest importance. He sees it as one
> of the most fundamental articles of faith. He
> maintains thereby that God the Lord is
> absolutely sovereign and that He alone
> determines who shall be saved. With this
> confession, as far as he is concerned, stands or
> falls the entire Reformed faith. By this
> confession, it is maintained that God is God,
> that no one is God except Him.[15]

The Protestant Reformed Churches have persevered
in warding off the hyper-Calvinistic danger on the right
hand even as they did battle with Arminianism on the
left hand. In the early 1950s, through a fierce, internal
struggle, they rejected the doctrine of a conditional
covenant, a doctrine essentially the same as that of the
well-meant offer of salvation. At that time, they adopted
"A Brief Declaration of Principles" in which they confessed the doctrine of God's unconditional covenant of
grace and the truth of the unconditional promise of the
gospel. Even though they had their eye on the teaching
that the preaching is a conditional promise of God to all
hearers, a teaching found at that time within their own
denomination, they did not react by swinging over to
the other, hyper-Calvinistic extreme. In the very "Declaration" in which they condemned the doctrine of a
conditional promise, they steadfastly confessed that the
preaching of the (particular) promise is and must be
promiscuous and that the preaching calls all hearers to
repent and believe:

This *preaching* of the particular promise is

---

15. Ibid., "Foreword."

promiscuous to all that hear the gospel with the *command,* not a condition, to repent and believe.

And we maintain:

1. That God surely and infallibly fulfills His promise to the elect.

2. The sure promise of God which He realizes in us as rational and moral creatures not only makes it impossible that we should not bring forth fruits of thankfulness but also confronts us with the obligation of love, to walk in a new and holy life, and constantly to watch unto prayer.

All those who are not thus disposed, who do not repent but walk in sin, are the objects of His just wrath and excluded from the Kingdom of Heaven.

That the preaching comes to all; and that God seriously commands to faith and repentance, and that to all those who come and believe He promises life and peace.[16]

It is indisputable that the Protestant Reformed Churches' rejection of a well-meant offer and a conditional promise is not and never was motivated by hyper-Calvinism, that is, by a refusal to preach the gospel to every creature, a refusal to call every hearer to repentance and faith, and a refusal to proclaim to everyone the promise that whoever believes shall be saved. This was simply not the issue. Rather, the issue in the doctrine of a well-meant offer of the gospel is this: does God love

16. This "Declaration of Principles" is found in *The Church Order of the Protestant Reformed Churches and Constitutions of Standing Synodical Committees, Rules and Regulations, Formulae, By-laws* (published March 1947; revised and updated 1992), pp. 109-134.

and have a gracious attitude towards everyone who hears the preaching, and does He in the preaching desire to save everyone? As Hoeksema never wearied of asking, "What grace does the reprobate receive in the preaching?"

Just as it is misrepresentation to present Hoeksema's rejection of the offer as hyper-Calvinism, so it is nothing but a caricature to portray him and others who deny the offer as men who, by virtue of their rejection of the offer, lack the fervent ardor of the apostle Paul to gain and save many (I Cor. 9:19ff.), as men who are unable or unwilling to beseech others to be reconciled to God (II Cor. 5:20), and as men who take delight in preaching men to hell. Invariably, critics of his opposition to the offer have painted Hoeksema in these colors. Essentially, it is nothing more or less than the hoary Arminian calumny of the Reformed preacher because of his confession of the doctrine of reprobation. Everything that has been said along these lines about those who deny that God is gracious to all in the preaching holds with equal validity for those who confess reprobation.

But the portrayal is false, if it is not malicious. In the spirit of Calvin, who called the doctrine of reprobation the *"decretum horrible"*[17] (without for a moment ceasing to confess and publicly proclaim it), Hoeksema admonished his students never to take the word "reprobation"

---

17. John Calvin, *Institutes of the Christian Religion*, tr. Henry Beveridge (Grand Rapids: Wm. B. Eerdmans Publishing Company, 1957), 3.23.7. Calvin is speaking of God's decree that some men perish eternally through the fall of Adam, which God ordained. "Here the most loquacious tongues must be dumb. The decree, I admit, is dreadful; and yet it is impossible to deny that God foreknew what the end of man was to be before he made him, and foreknew, because he had so ordained by his decree."

on their lips in their preaching and teaching without trembling. In his book, *Een Kracht Gods*, after he has explained II Corinthians 2:14-16, Hoeksema wrote:

> From a human viewpoint, a preacher may want to save all who are in his audience, and want to take them with him to heaven. Certainly he will not, cannot, and may not seek to be a savor of death unto death. His calling is to be a good savor of Christ, and to preach God's Word faithfully. If he does this, his task is fulfilled, and he leaves the outcome to the Lord.

But the faithful preacher also "prepared himself to be willing to be a savor of death unto death, as well as a savor of life unto life. For such is the will of God. And only in this way is he always a conqueror."[18]

That which is objectionable in the "free offer of the gospel," or "well-meant gospel offer," is not the teaching that the church must preach the gospel to everyone and must call all hearers to faith in Jesus Christ. But the error of the doctrine of the offer, and the reason why a Reformed man must repudiate it, is its teaching that the grace of God in Jesus Christ, grace that is saving in character, is directed to all men in the preaching of the gospel. Inherent in the offer of the gospel is the notion that God loves and desires to save all men; the notion that the preaching of the gospel is God's grace to all men, an expression of God's love to all men, and an attempt by God to save all men; and the notion that salvation is dependent upon man's acceptance of the offered salva-

---

18. Hoeksema, *Een Kracht Gods*, p. 96.

tion, that is, that salvation depends upon the free will of
the sinner.[19]

The first two of these elements are openly confessed
by the proponents of the offer. In the first of the three
points of common grace of 1924, the Christian Reformed
Church expressed the following:

> Relative to the first point which concerns the
> favorable attitude of God towards humanity
> in general and not only towards the elect,
> synod declares it to be established according
> to Scripture and the Confession that, apart
> from the saving grace of God shown only to
> those that are elect unto eternal life, there is
> also a certain favor or grace of God which He
> shows to His creatures in general. This is
> evident from the Scriptural passages quoted
> and from the Canons of Dordrecht, II, 5 and
> III, IV, 8, 9, which deal with the general offer
> of the Gospel, while it also appears from the
> citations made from Reformed writers of the
> most flourishing period of Reformed Theology
> that our Reformed writers from the past
> favored this view.[20]

---

19. In his book, *Een Kracht Gods Tot Zaligheid,* Hoeksema listed
four objectionable elements in the idea of an offer of salvation.
First, the offer teaches that God wills and desires to give grace to,
or save, all men. Second, it teaches that God actually possesses
salvation for all, that is, that Christ's atonement was universal.
Third, it holds that God plainly reveals that it is His intention to
give His grace to all. Fourth, it implies that salvation is conditioned
by the free will of the sinner. Each of these elements "conflicts with
the Reformed truth." The offer and the Reformed truth "are
mutually exclusive" (pp. 8-13).
20. *Acta Der Synode 1924 Van De Christelijke Gereformeerde
Kerk,* pp. 145, 146. The translation given here is that of H.
Hoeksema in his *The Protestant Reformed Churches in America,*

The Orthodox Presbyterian Church confessed the same doctrine, if anything more plainly and more boldly when in 1948 it adopted the doctrinal study of Professors John Murray and Ned B. Stonehouse on "the free offer of the gospel":

> ... there is in God a benevolent lovingkindness towards the repentance and salvation of even those whom he has not decreed to save. This pleasure, will, desire is expressed in the universal call to repentance.... The full and free offer of the gospel is a grace bestowed upon all. Such grace is necessarily a manifestation of love or lovingkindness in the heart of God, and this lovingkindness is revealed to be of a character or kind that is correspondent with the grace bestowed. The grace offered is nothing less than salvation in its richness and fulness. The love or lovingkindness that lies back of that offer is not anything less; it is the will to that salvation. In other words, it is Christ in all the glory of his person and in all the perfection of his finished work whom God offers in the gospel. The loving and benevolent will that is the

---

2nd ed. (Grand Rapids: n.p., 1947), p. 317. The original Dutch of the first point is as follows: *"Aangaande het eerste punt, rakende* de gunstige gezindheid Gods jegens de menschheid in het algemeen, en niet alleen jegens de uitverkorenen, *spreekt de Synode uit dat volgens Schrift en Confessie het vaststaat, dat er, behalve de zaligmakende genade Gods bewezen alleen aan de uitverkorenen ten eeuwigen leven, ook een zekere gunst of genade Gods is, die Hij betoont aan Zijn schepselen in het algemeen. Dit blijkt uit de aangehaalde Schriftuurplaatsen en uit de Dordtsche Leerregels II, 5, en III en IV, 8 en 9, waar gehandeld wordt van de algemeene aanbieding des Evangelies; terwijl het uit de aangehaalde uitspraken van Geref. schrijvers uit den bloeitijd der Geref. theologie bovendien blijkt, dat onze Gereformeerde vaderen van oudsher dit gevoelen hebben voorgestaan."*

> source of that offer and that grounds its
> veracity and reality is the will to the possession
> of Christ and the enjoyment of the salvation
> that resides in him.[21]

The free offer, according to those who hold to it, is the grace of God to all men in the preaching of the gospel, grace rooted in God's love for all men. This grace must be conceived of as God's one, saving grace. For it is grace that desires men's salvation; it is grace revealed in the preaching of the gospel of Christ crucified; and it is grace that offers Christ and the riches of salvation to men.

In the first point of common grace, the Christian Reformed Church identified the grace manifested in the offer as a "certain favor or grace of God" which is to be distinguished from "the saving grace of God shown only to those that are elect." Following the lead of Abraham Kuyper, who, however, did not make common grace a favor of God which desired the salvation of all humanity and which offered all men salvation, the Christian Reformed Church distinguished two graces of God, "common grace" and "special (saving) grace." The former was viewed as a favor that gives all men earthly blessings, e.g., health, and the latter was viewed as the favor of God that gives the elect salvation.

In the past, the Christian Reformed Church has attempted to defend its doctrine of the offer by claiming that it is the revelation of God's common grace, not His special, saving grace. But the grace of God expressed in the well-meant offer is saving grace, not some "common

---

21. The *Minutes* of the Fifteenth General Assembly of the Orthodox Presbyterian Church, 1948, Appendix, pp. 51-63. This report of a committee has been printed as a booklet, *The Free Offer of the Gospel* (n.p., n.d.). The quotation is found on page 27 of the booklet.

grace." Even though it is grace that fails to save many to whom it is directed, it is as to its character the saving grace of God in Jesus Christ. It is not a grace that gives rain, sunshine, health, and wealth, but a grace that desires a man's salvation and that well-meaningly offers a man Christ and Him crucified. It is sheer absurdity to make the offer of the gospel an expression of a non-saving "common grace." It is simply a principle that will work its way out, regardless of all foolish distinctions, that the grace of God in the blessed gospel is saving grace. Besides, the fact of the matter is, Abraham Kuyper to the contrary notwithstanding, that the Scriptures know of only one grace of God and one love of God, His grace and love in Jesus Christ. This is the grace and this is the love revealed in the gospel.

The doctrine of the offer, therefore, teaches that the love of God in Christ is universal. Apart from all other considerations, this is the denial of the Reformed, biblical doctrine of election and the sell-out of the Reformed faith to Arminianism. For the meaning of the doctrine of election is that the love of God in Christ is eternally directed towards some definite, particular men, willing their salvation and efficaciously accomplishing it. Election is simply the choosing love of God (Deut. 7:6-8; Rom. 8:28-39). Universal love is universal election, and that was the position of the Arminians.

Since the offer maintains that God's grace is directed to all men in the preaching, it is the denial of the efficacy or sovereignty of grace, that which the fourth of the so-called Five Points of Calvinism calls "the irresistibility of grace." For the doctrine of the offer does admit that many of those to whom God is gracious in the preaching are not saved.

Here the doctrine of the offer most clearly shows itself to be the resurrection of the old Arminian heresy

in the Reformed camp. The pivotal point in the controversy between the Reformed faith and Arminianism at
the time of the Synod of Dordt was the Arminian denial
of the sovereignty of grace. Basic to the Arminian
position was their teaching that God's grace is given to
all men, not sovereignly to save them but merely to
enable them to choose salvation, if they willed. At this
crucial juncture — the actual salvation of a man —
everything depends upon the man himself, upon his
exercise of his free will. And the whole of Arminian
theology is built on this rotten foundation: election, the
atonement, and final salvation are conditioned by the
free will of the sinner.[22]

The Synod of Dordt laid waste the entire Arminian
system and maintained the gospel of gracious salvation
by confessing with the Scriptures that the grace of God,
both as an attitude in God and as His power in men, does
not enable a man to be saved, does not merely make
salvation possible, but efficaciously saves everyone
towards whom it is directed and in whom it is worked.
The Synod denied "that after God has performed his
part, it still remains in the power of man to be regenerated or not to be regenerated, to be converted or to
continue unconverted" (Canons, III, IV/12). Rather, the

22. The significance at Dordt of the truth of sovereign, irresistible
grace is indicated in Carl Bangs' book, sympathetic to the Arminians,
Arminius (Nashville: Abingdon Press, 1971). Presbyterian theologian Benjamin B. Warfield has observed that "the doctrine of
monergistic regeneration — or as it was phrased by the older
theologians, of 'irresistible grace' or 'effectual calling' — is the
hinge of the Calvinistic soteriology, and lies much more deeply
embedded in the system than the doctrine of predestination itself
which is popularly looked upon as its hall-mark" (Benjamin B.
Warfield, *Calvin and Calvinism,* New York: Oxford University
Press, 1931, p. 359).

work of grace is such "that all in whose heart God works in this marvellous manner, are certainly, infallibly, and effectually regenerated and do actually believe." The Canons go on to say:

> Faith is therefore to be considered as the gift of God, not on account of its being offered by God to man, to be accepted or rejected at his pleasure; but because it is in reality conferred, breathed, and infused into him; or even because God bestows the power or ability to believe, and then expects that man should by the exercise of his own free will, consent to the terms of salvation, and actually believe in Christ; but because he who works in man both to will and to do, and indeed all things in all, produces both the will to believe, and the act of believing also (III, IV/14).

Salvation by grace, as taught in Ephesians 2:1-10, means that dead sinners are quickened by the almighty power of God, that is, sovereign grace. This implies, as Ephesians 1 explicitly teaches, that God's favorable attitude, His will to save, that is, His grace, is directed towards some particular men, namely, the elect. In this light the Arminian notions of conditional election and an atonement whose application depends on the sinner's decision are also exposed as fraudulent. The gospel is the good news of sovereign, particular grace. The doctrine of the well-meant offer is opposed to this.

The only alternative to the truth of sovereign grace is the teaching that salvation depends upon the free will of the sinner. This is another aspect of the theory of the offer to which a Reformed man objects. We appreciate the fact that in the past defenders of the offer within the Reformed sphere have vehemently repudiated free will, despite the inconsistency of their repudiation with the doctrine of the offer itself. Nevertheless, the teaching of free will is necessarily implied in the doctrine of the offer and can be repudiated only by repudiating the offer itself.

First, the idea of the concept "offer" in the context of a universal love of God and a desire of God to save everyone is that salvation depends upon the sinner's acceptance or rejection of the offer. In the past, the word "offer" from the Latin word *"offero"* was used by Reformed men to describe God's activity in the preaching of the gospel because the word has originally the meaning "bring to (someone)," "present (something or someone to somebody)." All Reformed men hold that Christ is presented in the preaching to everyone who hears the preaching. In this sense He is "offered" in the gospel. Calvin used "offer" in this sense, as do the Canons of Dordt: "It is not the fault of the gospel, nor of Christ, offered therein ... that those who are called by the ministry of the word, refuse to come ..." (III, IV/9). But this is not the meaning of the word when it is used in connection with a universal love of God and a desire of God to save everybody.[23]

Second, the truth of sovereign grace has only one alternative: salvation dependent on man's willing or

---

23. Others have noted with regard to Calvin's use of "offer" that *"offero"* meant "to present, to exhibit or set forth" (see *Calvin's Calvinism*, tr. Henry Cole, Grand Rapids: Wm. B. Eerdmans Publishing Co., 1950; repr., Grand Rapids: Reformed Free Publishing Association, n.d., p. 31, footnote). Although our quarrel with the offer is not a quibbling over words, the word "offer" should be dropped from the Reformed vocabulary. Not a biblical term, it is today so loaded with Arminian connotations that it is no longer serviceable. Instead of an offer of the gospel, we should speak of the call of the gospel as the Scriptures do.

running (see Rom. 9:16). Since the doctrine of the offer denies the sovereignty of grace, it necessarily affirms that salvation is dependent on, or conditioned by, man's acceptance of the offer by his own free will. Faith is then generally viewed as man's all-important acceptance of the offer by his own free will.

In spite of the insistence of those in the Reformed sphere who defend the offer that they reject the doctrine of free will, concerning the sincerity of which we have no doubt in many cases, the doctrine of the well-meant offer contains the germ of that heresy and will, I predict, result in open ecclesiastical confession of free will where the offer reigns, just as it has already resulted in official ecclesiastical approval of universal atonement.

Certain steps are already being taken in the direction of a formal confession of free will by Reformed churches. One of these is the wide-spread representation of faith as a condition to salvation by Reformed theologians. Invariably, a defense of the offer of the gospel will stress that salvation is conditional and that the condition is man's faith. This is true of A.C. DeJong's defense of the well-meant offer against Hoeksema in his *The Well-Meant Gospel Offer*. In criticizing Hoeksema's denial of the offer, DeJong felt it necessary first of all to attack Hoeksema's contention that the covenant, the promise, and salvation are unconditional.[24] His own defense of the offer took the form of emphasizing that salvation is conditional: "For implicit in the concept of offer is the idea of conditionality"; "Hoeksema argues as if God does not will that his conditional offer be accepted."[25] The condition, of course, is faith. DeJong is representa-

---

24. A.C. DeJong, *Well-Meant Gospel Offer*, pp. 72ff.
25. Ibid., pp. 100, 123.

tive of all those who defend the offer.[26]

DeJong is correct when he states that the idea of conditionality is implicit in the concept of the offer. That God loves all and desires to save all, while not all are actually saved, implies that salvation depends upon man's fulfilling the condition of faith. That God saves by *offering* Christ and salvation to men implies that salvation depends upon the condition of accepting, that is, faith. But the biblical and Reformed doctrine is that salvation is unconditional. If the glorious truth "by grace ye are saved" does not mean this, it means nothing. The Reformed doctrine of "unconditional election" explicitly describes salvation as "unconditional." Election is the source and foundation of all salvation. If election is unconditional, so also are the atonement, regeneration, sanctification, preservation, and glorification. It is the creedal Reformed position, not the private speculations of Herman Hoeksema, that salvation is unconditional — not conditional, not conditional and unconditional, but unconditional.

The Canons of Dordt reject any and every form of conditional salvation, especially the form that makes faith a condition, in the rejection of errors under Head I:

> ... the Synod rejects the errors of those ... who teach ... that He (God) chose out of all possible conditions ... the act of faith which from its very nature is undeserving ... as a condition of salvation....
>
> ... the Synod rejects the errors of those ... who

---

26. For a defense of the offer by means, necessarily, of a defense of a conditional covenant and conditional salvation from a different quarter, see the Anglican theologian Peter Toon, *The Emergence of Hyper-Calvinism in English Nonconformity,* pp. 59, 60.

> teach ... that ... faith, the obedience of faith,
> holiness, godliness and perseverance are not
> fruits of the unchangeable election unto glory,
> but are conditions....

A condition of salvation is an act that man must and can perform of himself and an act upon which salvation depends. A conditional salvation is in principle a salvation dependent upon the free will of man. If the idea of conditionality is implied in the concept of the offer, there is nothing to be done with the concept of the offer than to cast it out of the Reformed tent like an Ishmael. But the Reformed churches today are permeated with the notion that man's faith is the condition unto salvation. Thus, they are already on the way to a formal confession of free will.

Another step in that direction is taken when Reformed theologians, in the midst of their defense of a well-meant offer, answer the question "Why, if God loves and desires to save all men, are not all men saved?" by appealing to a "mystery." This was the answer of Harold Dekker, professor of missions in Calvin Seminary, in the course of his argument for universal atonement on the basis of the doctrine of the well-meant offer of the gospel. Having said that God loves all men with a redemptive love and that Christ died for all men, he asked, "If God loves all men with a redemptive love, how is it that not all men are saved?"[27]

In fairness to Dekker, he did not take the last step into full-fledged Arminianism by adopting free will. This leaves him in a curious position. On the one hand, he embraces the Arminian doctrine of universal election ("God loves all men with a redemptive love") and the

---

27. Harold Dekker, "God's Love for Sinners — One or Two?" *Reformed Journal* 13 (March 1963), p. 15.

Arminian doctrine of resistible grace (God's grace, which Dekker correctly insists is one — the saving grace in Christ — fails to save many towards whom it is directed). On the other hand, he stops short of maintaining the Arminian doctrine of free will, which is the teaching on which all of the others hinge.

One likes to say to Dekker, "Look here, your entire theology demands the doctrine of free will. If you maintain your theology of universal redemptive love, universal atonement, and universal grace in the preaching, take the last step too so that everybody knows what is what. But if you seriously hesitate to affirm free will, the only alternative is God's sovereign salvation of some particular sinners: He freely and sovereignly saves some in distinction from others for no other reason than His own good pleasure. But this is the utter destruction of your doctrines of universal election and universal atonement. If you maintain salvation by sovereign grace, in distinction from free will, what have you gained by your doctrines of universal election and universal atonement? You can now preach to all men that God loves them with a redemptive love and that Christ died for them to save them from their sins, but at the same time you must whisper to yourself, 'But He will actually save only some of you and He will not save others of you according to His own sovereign will.' What you whisper to yourself makes the message of universal love, universal atonement, and a universal desire to save, which you proclaim loudly, a fraud."

Even though Dekker did not give free will as the answer to the question "How is it that not all men are saved?" the answer that he did give was a step in the wrong direction. Dekker's answer was: "Let us ... (leave) the unexplainable where it belongs — in the infinite mystery of the heart of Him who is himself love.

On the side of divine sovereignty, then, there is mystery. On the side of human responsibility, however, there is no mystery at all. The answer is plainly a matter of unbelief."[28]

It is true that, as concerns man's responsibility, the reason why many perish is their own unbelief. The fault is man's own. But it is not true, as regards God's sovereignty, that one can refer only to the mystery. The Scriptures teach that the explanation why not all men are saved is that God has eternally reprobated some men, eternally decreeing that they perish in their sins, and that God, according to His decree, does not bestow faith upon them but hardens them in sin. In Romans 9, in explanation of the fact that some in Israel were saved and others were not (vv. 6-8), Paul plainly teaches that God loved and chose some but hated and reprobated others (vv. 11-13). According to this double predestination, God has mercy on some but hardens the others (v. 18). The reason why there are "vessels of mercy ... afore prepared unto glory" (v. 23) is that the Potter has "power over the clay ... to make one vessel unto honour" (v. 21). The reason why there are "vessels of wrath fitted to destruction" (v. 22) is that the Potter has power also "to make ... another (vessel) unto dishonour" (v. 21).

In the old dispensation, salvation was enjoyed by one nation while all the other nations perished. The explanation is not shrouded in "mystery." Rather, the explanation is the sovereign, discriminating actions of Jehovah: "He sheweth his word unto Jacob, his statutes and his judgments unto Israel. He hath not dealt so with any nation..." (Ps. 147:19, 20).

Christ did not hesitate to reveal to the unbelieving Jews that "ye believe not, because ye are not of my

28. Ibid., p. 15.

sheep..." (John 10:26). On the other hand, the reason why other men do believe and have eternal life is that they are Jesus' sheep, given to Him of the Father in divine election (vv. 27-29).

The Canons of Dordt explain why some men are saved and others are not: some receive the gift of faith from God, and others do not receive it. And "that some receive the gift of faith from God, and others do not receive it proceeds from God's eternal decree" (I/6).

Why God has chosen to save some in distinction from others is indeed a mystery, the mystery of the free and sovereign grace of God which we who are saved can only adore. But there is an answer to the question "Why are some saved, while others are not saved?" That answer is the sovereignty of God in predestination. Such an answer is the death-blow to free will. To refuse to give this answer but instead to speak of a "mystery" is to open up the way to a future solving of the "mystery" in terms of the free will of man. Not only is this answer the death-blow to free will, but it is also the death-blow to universal love, universal atonement, and a universal desire to save, that is, to the offer of the gospel.

In the meantime, before there is official adoption of free will, free will is widely preached and taught in Reformed churches. When ministers *practice* the offer of the gospel, proclaiming to their hearers that God loves them all, desires the salvation of everybody, and now offers them salvation, they are telling the people that salvation depends upon man's decision for Christ. This is the message that comes through to the people loudly and clearly, even though there is no official decision of the church approving free will and even though the preacher does not explicitly say as many today do, "Now it is up to you."

Rejection of the well-meant offer is not hyper-Calvinism, but Calvinism. The well-meant offer is an Arminian intruder in the Reformed camp. The offer of the gospel leaves tracks wherever it goes that plainly identify it as Arminianism, not Calvinism. One of these is the denial of reprobation. Invariably, the defense and practice of the offer is attended by a silencing or corrupting of the Reformed doctrine of reprobation.

A striking example of the perversion of the doctrine of reprobation in the interests of the offer of the gospel is A.C. DeJong's *The Well-Meant Gospel Offer.* DeJong was concerned to defend the well-meant offer. But he had to face Hoeksema's objection that the doctrine of reprobation exactly denies that God is gracious to all, desires the salvation of all, and well-meaningly offers Christ to all in the preaching. DeJong's solution was to oppose "Hoeksema's doctrine of reprobation." "Hoeksema's doctrine of reprobation renders the reliability of God's unsimulated call to salvation disputable." "Our chief objection to Hoeksema's view of reprobation is that it transforms the gospel into a message which renders suspect the reliability of God's will to save as this is revealed in the call to faith, in the conditional offer of salvation."

It soon becomes evident, however, that DeJong is not opposed to some private view of Herman Hoeksema, but to the historic, creedal doctrine of reprobation of the Reformed faith. According to DeJong, reprobation has to do with God's decision to "condemn those who wilfully and persistently oppose his word which is given and spoken for the purpose of salvation." DeJong's departure from the Reformed doctrine of reprobation and his subscription to the classic Arminian view of reprobation become apparent when he describes reprobation thus: "No one disbelieves because he is a reprobate. He is a reprobate because he does not want to

believe, because he wills to live without God, and
because he resists the redemptive will of God revealed
in the gospel call."[29]

Reprobation on this view is God's decree that those
men who persistently reject the offer of the gospel shall
be damned. The decree of reprobation is a conditional
decree, a decree dependent upon the unbelief of men in
the face of God's desire and attempt to save them.[30]

That was the view of reprobation which the
Arminians attempted to introduce into the Reformed
churches in the seventeenth century. Reprobation conditioned by unbelief was the counterpart of an election
conditioned by faith in the first article of the Arminian
"Remonstrance of 1610": "(reprobation is God's decree)
to leave the incorrigible and unbelieving in sin and
under wrath and condemn them...."[31] In the "Opinions"
which they submitted to the Synod of Dordt, the
Arminians described reprobation in this way: "Rejection from eternal life is made on the basis of a consideration of antecedent unbelief and perseverance in unbelief; not, however, apart from a consideration of ante-

---

29. A.C. DeJong, *Well-Meant Gospel Offer*, pp. 122, 123, 130.
30. This view of reprobation is by this time widespread in Reformed churches. The influential Berkouwer advanced it in his
Divine Election, particularly pp. 172-217. James Daane gives
expression to it in his *The Freedom of God* (Grand Rapids: Wm. B.
Eerdmans Publishing Co., 1973): "any doctrine of reprobation is
illegitimate by biblical standards *except that which biblical teaching
sanctions:* that he who rejects God, God rejects" (p. 200). This view
of reprobation brings these men into irreconcilable conflict with the
Canons, as they well know. This is one of the reasons for their
concomitant attack on the authority of the creeds and on the
Formula of Subscription.
31. *Crisis in the Reformed Churches: Essays in Commemoration
of the Great Synod of Dort, 1618-19,* ed. Peter Y. DeJong (Grand
Rapids: Reformed Fellowship, Inc., 1968), p. 208.

cedent unbelief and perseverance in unbelief."[32]

The Synod of Dordt rejected as heretical the view that reprobation is merely God's indefinite decree to damn whoever happens to reject the offer of the gospel and the view that reprobation is God's decree to damn certain men because of foreseen unbelief. In Article VIII of the "Rejection of Errors" under the first head of doctrine, the synod rejected the errors of those "Who teach: That God simply by virtue of his righteous will, did not decide either to leave anyone in the fall of Adam and in the common state of sin and condemnation, or to pass anyone by in the communication of grace which is necessary for faith and conversion...." In support of reprobation "simply by virtue of His righteous will" and against a doctrine of conditional reprobation, the Synod quoted Romans 9:18, Matthew 13:11, and Matthew 11:25, 26.

The Reformed doctrine of reprobation is that God has eternally decreed "out of His sovereign, most just, irreprehensible and unchangeable good pleasure" that certain, definite members of the human race will not be saved by Him, but that they shall perish in their unbelief and other sins (Canons, I/15). Reprobation is God's eternal decree that the destiny of certain men shall be everlasting death, whether one views it as God's passing those men by with the grace of election or as the determination to damn.

The cause of this decree is not the unbelief and disobedience of the reprobated, but the sovereign good pleasure of the decreeing God. Reprobation is not a conditional but an unconditional decree. That this is so

---

32. The eighth of the Remonstrant, or Arminian, opinions regarding the decree of predestination (see *Crisis in the Reformed Churches,* ed. Peter Y. DeJong, pp. 223, 224).

is evident from the Canons. According to the Canons, I/15, reprobation is the decree "not to bestow upon them saving faith and the grace of conversion." If reprobation is the decree not to give a man faith, it is patently false to say that unbelief is the cause of reprobation. That would be the same as to say that my decision not to give a beggar a quarter is due to the beggar's not having a quarter. That reprobation is an unconditional decree is also plain from the fact that if unbelief were the cause of reprobation, all men would have been reprobated, and none would have been elected, for all men are equally unbelieving and disobedient.

The Scriptures teach that reprobation is God's sovereign, unconditional decree to damn some sinners. This is the inescapable implication of the biblical doctrine that God has unconditionally chosen some men, not all, unto eternal life. This is also the explicit teaching of the Scriptures. In Romans 9 Paul ascribes God's hardening of some unto damnation simply to God's will (v. 18) and finds in the sovereignty of the Potter the authority both to make a vessel unto honor and to make a vessel unto dishonor from the same lump of clay (vv. 21-23).

It is not at all surprising that advocates of the free offer oppose the Reformed doctrine of reprobation, for reprobation is the exact, explicit denial that God loves all men, desires to save all men, and conditionally offers them salvation. Reprobation asserts that God eternally hates some men; has immutably decreed their damnation; and has determined to withhold from them Christ, grace, faith, and salvation. The Reformed doctrine of reprobation and the theology of the well-meant offer are diametrical opposites.[33] To affirm the offer is to deny reprobation.

---

33. Men like to throw up the smokescreen that it is only the

But a denial of reprobation is necessarily also a denial of election. If reprobation is made a conditional decree, the decree to condemn whoever rejects the offer, election becomes a conditional decree also, the decree to save whoever accepts the offer. This is the goal that Arminian theology and the proud heart of man singlemindedly pursue, for this is the blasphemous claim that we save ourselves. The attack on election is out in the open today in the Reformed sphere. When a Reformed theologian of vast erudition can write a 330-page book on election without ever once saying that God elected certain, particular men in distinction from others, as G.C. Berkouwer did in *Divine Election,* the cat is out of the bag. When, in addition, Reformed theologians warn against thinking of any reprobation in connection with election, it is apparent to him with even the least sensitive of "Reformed antennae" that a rampaging universalism is destroying the Reformed doctrine of election.[34]

---

supralapsarian view of reprobation that rules out the well-meant offer, just as they like to disguise their opposition to reprobation as opposition to supralapsarianism ("Hoeksema's doctrine of reprobation"). The last word has not been spoken in the brotherly debate within the Reformed camp over infra- and supralapsarianism. But this difference has absolutely no bearing on the issue of the offer. It is the Reformed doctrine of reprobation, whether viewed in an infra- or in a supralapsarian manner, that condemns the offer and that must give place where the offer is found.

34. See Lewis B. Smedes, *All Things Made New* (Grand Rapids: Wm. B. Eerdmans Publishing Co., 1970): "We will never think of election as a grace-less, love-less decree to select some individuals for heaven and to reject other individuals for hell. The election in Christ is not a matter of numbers" (pp. 123, 124). His description of the Reformed doctrine of election is a caricature, but his point is clear: there is no reprobation, and election is election of every man. See also James Daane's *The Freedom of God:* "The gracious elective

Other zealous defenders of the offer handle the problem of the opposition between the doctrine of the offer and reprobation by studiously ignoring reprobation. The silence on reprobation in many Reformed pulpits and in the writings of many Calvinistic Baptists is deafening. It must be very difficult to read the Bible without seeing reprobation. How does one manage it as he reads the Old Testament with its message of God's choice of one nation unto life out of many nations left to perish in their sin? How can one remain ignorant of reprobation when he reads freely in the New Testament —Matthew 11:25-27, John 10, Romans 9, I Peter 2:8, Jude 4? One could only conclude from the silence of many on reprobation that there is no reprobation. But if there is no reprobation, neither is there any election.

The recourse of some to "the mystery" to solve the problem of the contradiction between the free offer and the Reformed doctrine of reprobation is both desperate and erroneous. Such like to speak of the paradox of God's two wills: His will to save and His will not to save the same man. For God to love and to hate the same man, to desire to save and to reprobate the same man, to be gracious in the preaching of the gospel towards and to harden the same man is sheer contradiction. The reality of the twofold will of God is quite different. It has to do with the fact that God at the same time decrees that a man shall not be saved (the will of God's decree) and commands that man to repent and believe (the will of God's precept). The serious, external call of the gospel does justice to both of these aspects of God's will, but the offer of the gospel places a contradiction in God.

... act of God ... has no corresponding negative power that posits a reprobative counterpart.... Election ... has no counterpart, *not even a negative reprobative counterpart*" (p. 200).

Another Arminian footprint of the well-meant offer is the teaching of universal atonement. Herman Hoeksema prophesied that "those that preach a well-meaning offer of God to all men, must and will ultimately embrace the doctrine of universal atonement also." The ground for this confident prophecy was: "God's well-meaning 'offer' of salvation cannot possibly be wider in scope than the objective satisfaction and justification of the cross of Christ."[35] In the 1960s, through the writings of Harold Dekker, professor of missions in its seminary, the Christian Reformed Church approved, if it did not adopt, the doctrine of universal atonement. What made this so significant was the fact that Dekker grounded his doctrine of universal atonement in the doctrine of the well-meant offer. Arguing for a universal love of God and a universal atonement, he wrote:

> The universal love of God is also revealed in His invitation of the gospel, sincerely extended to all without reservation of limitation.
>
> Moreover, God's sincere invitation of the gospel to all involves His desire that it be accepted by all.
>
> ... is the salvation which the atonement provides *available* to all men? Indeed it is. Otherwise the well-meant offer of the gospel is a farce, for it then offers sincerely to all men

---

35. Herman Hoeksema, *The Death of the Son of God* (Grand Rapids: Wm. B. Eerdmans Publishing Co., 1946), pp. 112, 113. This volume and the other nine volumes in the series have been reprinted as *The Triple Knowledge: An Exposition of the Heidelberg Catechism,* 3 vols. (Grand Rapids: Reformed Free Publishing Association, 1970-72). The quotations are found in 1:542, 543.

what cannot be sincerely said to be available
to all.[36]

When his teaching of universal atonement was chal-
lenged, Dekker defended it with an appeal to the doctrine of the offer of the gospel adopted by the Christian
Reformed Church in the first point of common grace of
1924. In an article entitled "Redemptive Love and the
Gospel Offer" he wrote: "This article intends to set forth
the universal factors inherent in the well-meant offer of
the gospel. It carries one main thrust: *that the love of God
expressed in the gospel and its universal invitation is truly a
redemptive love and that the presentation of the gospel must
express this principle.*"[37]

Replying to critics who objected that he taught an
atonement which failed to save all those for whom it was
made, Dekker showed them that this was no different
from their teaching that God desired to save all but
failed to do so, that is, that universal atonement is really
no different from the well-meant offer of the gospel:

> Why are my critics unwilling to recognize a
> paradox between a universal atonement and
> a limited redemption when this is so plainly
> taught in the Bible? Why are they unwilling
> to recognize a paradox of a redemptive love
> which does not always redeem when this is so
> clearly the presentation of Scripture? Do they
> suppose that such paradoxes as these are any
> greater or any more difficult to accept than
> the paradox which they affirm of a God who

36. Harold Dekker, "God So Loved—All Men!" *Reformed Journal*
12 (December 1962), pp. 5, 7.
37. Harold Dekker, "Redemptive Love and the Gospel Offer,"
Reformed Journal 14 (January 1964), p. 8.

> sincerely desires the salvation of all men and
> yet does not save them all?[38]

Dekker proved conclusively that the doctrine of the offer implies universal atonement and universal election (for a universal redemptive love is really universal election), and the Christian Reformed Church, having said "A" in 1924, said "B" in the 1960s.

Our opposition to the offer of the gospel is not academic. Through the teaching and practice of the offer, Arminianism has flooded the Reformed churches. Today, a Reformed man cries out: "O God, the heathen are come into thine inheritance; thy holy temple have they defiled; they have laid Jerusalem on heaps" (Ps. 79:1).

The revivalistic, "soul-winning" mentality of free will has taken over among many Reformed people. The altar call, that johnny-come-lately innovation of Finney, an abomination before God and man, is widely practiced in Reformed churches. The evangelism of Billy Graham is revered, so that if one dares to call the message of Graham "the doctrine of Pelagius out of hell," as the Canons of Dordt do indeed call it, he is likely to be stoned as a blasphemer in the streets of Reformed Jerusalem. The children of the covenant are more and more viewed, not as covenant children to be reared in the truth but as potential converts who must make the decision for Christ. Reformed churches are wide open to the most blatant Arminian, "free willist," evangelistic societies, e.g., Campus Crusade for Christ. They are ravaged by ecumenical endeavors based on Arminian universalism, e.g., Key '73 and "Here's Life, America."

---

38. Harold Dekker, "Reply (to a letter)," *Reformed Journal* 14 (September 1964), p. 22.

Loosened from their moorings by Arminianism, they are swept by every wind of doctrine that finds salvation in man's feeling and experience, e.g., neo-Pentecostalism.

Even the Holy Scriptures are defiled. Reformed people, schools, and churches gladly receive, eagerly use, and enthusiastically distribute as the Bible a book that is nothing other than a man's revision of the Scriptures along the lines of Arminian theology. Kenneth Taylor's *The Living Bible,* in all its myriad forms, is the bible of Arminianism. Systematically, it corrupts those passages of Scripture which teach the sovereignty of God in salvation and damnation, so that they will teach the sovereignty of the will of man. With this book, the Remonstrants had routed the Synod of Dordt.[39]

If a Reformed man had done to the sacred Scriptures in the interest of the Reformed faith only one tenth of that which *The Living Bible* has done in the interest of Arminianism, he would have been drawn and quartered in every pulpit and religious paper in the land, and his bible would have been scorned at the book stores. As for *The Living Bible,* it is lavished with praise, and its sales are booming. Why? Because the spiritual leaders delude the people, so that they no longer know that salvation is not of him that willeth, nor of him that runneth, but of God Who showeth mercy, and the people love their delusion.

---

39. Acts 13:48 is made to read: "... and as many as wanted eternal life, believed." Romans 8:28 becomes: "And we know that all that happens to us is working for our good if we love God and are fitting into His plans." Romans 8:29 reads: "For from the very beginning God decided that those who came to Him—and all along He knew who would — should become like His Son...." I Peter 2:8b is rendered: "They will stumble because they will not listen to God's Word, nor obey it, and so this punishment must follow—that they will fall."

There is only one hope for Reformed men and Reformed churches, and only the sovereign grace of God can realize it — back to Calvinism: the old Calvinism of Dordt, of Calvin, of Augustine, of Paul. And this means the rooting out of the well-meant offer of the gospel.

Chapter 3
The Reformed Doctrine of the Call of the Gospel

The Reformed doctrine of the preaching of the gospel must sail between the Scylla of hyper-Calvinism and the Charybdis of Arminianism. On the one hand is the rock of hyper-Calvinism which denies that the call of the gospel comes in all seriousness to everyone who hears the preaching, elect and reprobate alike. On the other hand is the whirlpool of Arminianism which makes the preaching a well-meant offer of God to all who hear. The Reformed view and practice of preaching must neither be smashed on the one nor swallowed up by the other.

We have already defended the Reformed conception of preaching against hyper-Calvinism. It remains to give account of Reformed preaching against objections raised by those who maintain a free offer.

Those who advocate a well-meant offer of grace insist that the offer is essential for free, unfettered preaching, especially for preaching directed to the unconverted in missions. They argue that the denial of an offer inhibits missions, or evangelism, by restricting the call of the gospel. Their argument seems to be, first, that a church or preacher that does not believe that God is gracious to all men will not desire, or dare, to preach to all men; second, that this church or preacher will not have a message to bring to every man; and, third, that such a church or preacher will be unable to call every man, urgently and seriously, to repent of his sins and believe in Jesus Christ.

Through the years, this has been the defense of its

doctrine of the well-meant offer by the Christian Reformed Church. H.J. Kuiper was representative when he wrote: "One of the most serious aspects of the present denial of the doctrine of Common Grace is the denial of the general offer of salvation. It robs the gospel of its evangelical note. It is bound in time to create an attitude of religious passivism and fatalism which has been the curse of every church where the preaching of election was not counter-balanced by the proclamation of the sinner's responsibility and of God's sincere offer of salvation to all without discrimination."[1]

Lately, the Calvinistic Baptists have been echoing these charges. In his booklet *The Free Offer* Erroll Hulse calls the rejection of the offer "hyper-Calvinism," which denies that all men should be "invited" to come to Christ, denies that faith is a duty, minimizes the moral and spiritual responsibility of sinners, and threatens the church that succumbs to it with death.[2]

Significantly, Harold Dekker used precisely the same arguments when he pleaded for the implications of the well-meant offer: universal redemptive love and universal atonement. He wrote: "The doctrine of limited atonement ... impairs the principle of the universal love of God and tends to inhibit missionary spirit and activity."[3] This same thought he later expressed positively: "The conviction that God loves all men and that Christ died for all ... could revolutionize the missionary motivation and program of our Church and make us truly

---

1.   Kuiper, *The Three Points of Common Grace,* p. 13.
2.   Erroll Hulse, *The Free Offer: An Exposition of Common Grace and the Free Invitation of the Gospel* (Haywards Heath, Sussex, England: Carey Publications Ltd., 1973), pp. 14, 15.
3.   Dekker, "God So Loved — All Men!" p. 7.

effective in the evangelization of the United States and Canada."[4]

The various defenders of the offer of the gospel are agreed that, unless a church believes that God is gracious to all men and desires to save all men, it will not zealously carry out Christ's command to go into all the world and preach the gospel to every creature. Dekker merely brought out what was inherent in this position when he insisted that, unless a preacher can say to every man, "God loves you, and Christ died for you," it is impossible to do the work of missions. Essentially, this is the position that the basis of missions is universal grace.

Dekker's unambiguous, forthright defense of universal redemptive love and universal atonement in the name of missions was a singularly clear indication that the kindred defense of a well-meant offer as something indispensable for missions is nothing else than a variation of the old, old charge by the Pelagian-Roman Catholic-Arminian party that the Reformed doctrine of eternal, sovereign predestination, election and reprobation, destroys lively preaching, especially to those outside the church.

Now, it is indeed true that the Reformed faith denies —and the Pelagians, Roman Catholics, and Arminians have always understood this well, thus showing themselves wiser than many who claim the name Reformed today — that preaching in general and missions in particular have any basis in a love, or grace, of God for all men or a desire of God that all men be saved. But the Reformed faith has always repudiated as wholly groundless and totally false the allegation that this in any way

---

4. Harold Dekker, "Limited Atonement and Evangelism," *Reformed Journal* 14 (May-June 1964), p. 24.

hinders the full, free activity of preaching the gospel, whether that be preaching within the established church or preaching to the unconverted.

The proof of the Reformed position is evident to all. The apostle Paul was an avowed, ardent predestinarian, holding double predestination, election and reprobation (Rom. 9). As a predestinarian, he did not believe, nor did he ever preach, that God loved all men, was gracious to all men, and desired the salvation of all men, that is, he did not believe, teach, or give the well-meant offer of the gospel. On the contrary, the apostle believed and proclaimed that God loved and chose unto salvation some men, and some men only (Rom. 9:11-13; 21-24; 11:5), hating and reprobating others (Rom. 9:13; 21, 22). He taught that God is gracious only to the elect (Rom. 9:15; II Tim. 1:9), enduring, blinding, and hardening the others (Rom. 9:22; 9:18; 11:7). He held that the preaching of the gospel, so far from being grace to all hearers, is a savor of death unto death to some (II Cor. 2:15, 16), in accordance with God's purpose in bringing the Word to them, which purpose is not a saving purpose, but the purpose to render them inexcusable and harden them (Rom. 9:18; cf. also Jesus' words in John 12:37-41).

Paul did not regard the preaching of the gospel as an *offer* of salvation to everyone, directed to everyone in a universal love of God and providing everyone with a chance to be saved. Instead, he viewed the preaching of the gospel as the power of God unto salvation (Rom. 1:16), as the creative call of God that calls the things that be not as though they were (Rom. 4:17), and as the mighty voice of the risen Christ that raises the dead (II Tim. 1:10). Such a quickening, renewing, and enlightening power is the preaching *unto God's elect.* This is true, not merely because it turns out to be the case that only the elect are saved by the gospel, but because God in the sovereignty of His grace limits the gospel as a saving power to the elect. The preaching of the gospel as the power of God unto salvation is dependent on and governed by God's eternal decree of predestination. Romans 8:30 teaches this: "Moreover whom he did predestinate, them he also called." God sends the gospel as a saving power only to those whom He has predestinated to be conformed to the image of His Son, and the gospel efficaciously saves every one to whom it is so directed.

But this doctrine did not stand in the way of Paul's engaging, fervently and energetically, in the work of missions. (To state such an obvious truth seems faintly ridiculous — those who assail predestination and the Reformed faith as inimical to missions are responsible for this foolishness.) The greatest predestinarian was the greatest missionary, and he was the latter because he was the former. He went preaching the glad tidings to the ends of the earth, and he willingly endured every imaginable hardship in the course of this labor (recall the marvelous list of sufferings in II Corinthians 11), "for the elect's sake, that they may also obtain the salvation which is in Christ Jesus with eternal glory" (II Tim. 2:10).

Are we really to suppose that, when it came to missions, the apostle set aside the doctrine of predestination as a teaching irrelevant to missions at best or as a teaching detrimental to missions and embarrassing at worst, in order to ground the activity of missions in, and to motive the missionary by, notions of a universal love and grace of God and a desire of God to save all men, notions that are not merely extraneous to the doctrine of predestination but that are in direct conflict with it?

Is this, really, a Reformed man's defense of missions today: missions are possible *in spite of* predestination?

How utterly foreign to Paul's thought!

How demeaning to the doctrine of predestination!

How inherently *destructive* of the doctrine of predestination!

If lively, unfettered preaching, evangelism, and missions cannot find their solid foundation and dynamic impetus in predestination, then predestination has to go. Such is the Christian consciousness.

The basis for missions, for urgent proclamation of the gospel to all and sundry, is the theology of predestination. With this conviction, gotten from and strengthened by the Holy Scriptures, we proceed to give account of our denial of a well-meant offer in response to the charge that without a love of God for all and a desire of God to save all we destroy missions.

The foundation of the activity of preaching the gospel is God's eternal decree of predestination. The reason why God has the gospel preached both throughout the world in missions and in the established churches is that the elect may be saved to the praise of His grace. Because of election, there are many in the fallen human race among all nations who are God's people and who must be saved. Preachers must go into all the world to preach the gospel to every creature (Matt. 28:18-20; Mark 16:15-20) so that these elect may be brought to salvation. After the Spirit has converted them and gathered them into churches, the gospel must be preached in the churches in order to feed the sheep and to build up the body of Christ (Eph. 4:12ff.). Neither mission-preaching nor any other form of preaching is grounded in a love of God for all men and a desire of God that all men be saved. All preaching is grounded in the love of God for His chosen people. What motivates the church, what motivates a missionary, what motivates a pastor is the gathering, defense, and preservation out of the human race of the church chosen to everlasting life (Heidelberg Catechism, Question 54). This is a sufficient motive, leaving nothing to be desired.

The Scriptures teach that divine election — not a universal love of God or a desire that all be saved — is the basis and motivation of missions, indeed of all preaching. This is Jesus' teaching in John 10. The Good Shepherd causes His voice to be heard in the world. How Jesus emphasizes the importance of His voice in this chapter. His voice is simply the preached gospel in all ages. His voice, that is, the gospel, *saves*. It leads the sheep out (v. 3). It causes the sheep to follow Him (v. 4). It safeguards them from the strangers, thieves, and robbers who are bent on the sheep's destruction (vv. 5, 8). It brings the sheep into the fold (v. 16). It is the means by which Jesus gives His sheep eternal life (v. 28), preserving them from perishing. For salvation, the Word must be preached and heard. But one thing is abundantly plain: the reason for the voice of the Shepherd is "my sheep," that is, the gathering and preservation of those men and women whom the Father eternally gave to Jesus in His decree of election (v. 29). Jesus does not send out His voice because God loves all men and desires all men to be saved. In the human race, among all nations (v. 16), there are some who are sheep, in distinction from others who are not sheep (v. 26). This is due to predestination. The Shepherd comes for the sheep, to give His life for them (v. 11) and to call them (v. 3).

The entire Old Testament is proof that preaching is grounded in election. God showed His Word unto Jacob, not to any other nation (Ps. 147:19, 20). The reason was not that the other nations were less likely to respond with repentance and faith. On the contrary, Christ Himself said that if the mighty works done in the great cities of Israel had been done in Tyre and Sidon, "they would have repented long ago in sackcloth and ashes," and that if they had been done in Sodom, "it would have remained until this day" (Matt. 11:20-24). But the reason why God gave His Word to Israel was that He had chosen Israel to be a special people unto Himself above all people that are upon the face of the earth (Deut. 7:6ff.).

That the work of missions is based on election is plain from the New Testament. According to Acts 18:10, the Lord encourages Paul to labor in Corinth by telling him in a vision: "For I am with thee, and no man shall set on thee to hurt thee: for I have much people in this city." Before Paul and the gospel ever got to Corinth, the Lord had much people there by virtue of God's election of many in that city. The reason why Paul was sent there to preach and the reason why he had to remain there preaching, in the face of opposition, was the salvation of the elect in that city. Paul knew very well that God did not love all the Corinthians and that God did not desire to save all the inhabitants of that city. Nothing of the sort motivated him to preach the gospel as a missionary. But he knew himself to be the instrument by whom the Lord gathered His people.

This relationship between election and preaching is set forth in all of the passages of Scripture that base the calling upon election. Romans 8:30 teaches that God calls the predestinated, or elect. II Thessalonians 2:13, 14 says that it is those who are beloved of the Lord and chosen from the beginning whom God calls by the gospel. II Timothy 1:9 states that people are called "according to his own purpose and grace, which was given us in Christ Jesus before the world began."

It is established, first of all, then, that the ground and motivation of all preaching, including missions, is election, not a grace of God for all. Missions, or evangelism, needs no "boost" from universal grace. Let him who still insists on bolstering missions with his fictitious grace of God for all men and divine desire that all be saved beware lest he, like Uzzah, be found "assisting" the ark of God, which needs no assistance, with unclean hands.

The means by which God *saves* the elect is the preaching of the gospel. The elect must be *saved*, that is, delivered from the spiritual death into which, like all the other members of the human race, they are conceived and born (Eph. 2:1-3) and translated into the kingdom of God's dear Son (Col. 1:13). They must have their eyes opened and must be turned from darkness to light and from the power of Satan to God, so that they may receive forgiveness of sins and inheritance among them which are sanctified by faith in Jesus Christ (Acts 26:18). They must be converted (Acts 3:19). They must be drawn to Christ in Whom is life and apart from Whom is death (John 6:44; Matt. 11:28). They must be made to believe on Jesus Christ (Acts 16:30, 31; 20:21) with the true and living faith through which they are justified (Rom. 3:28) and sanctified (Acts 26:18). Having been converted, they must be converted daily (Heidelberg Catechism, L.D. 33); nourished (I Pet. 2:2); preserved in the faith (I Pet. 1:5); and edified (Eph. 4:12). All of this salvation God accomplishes by the preaching of the gospel.

This is the confession of the Reformed faith. The Canons of Dordt begin, in the opening articles of the first head, by stating the good news that God in His love in Jesus Christ has determined to deliver some of the fallen, guilty, and depraved sons of Adam out of their sin, condemnation, and death (I/1, 2). Deliverance from perishing and the enjoyment of eternal life come through faith (I/2). "And that men may be brought to believe, God mercifully sends the messengers of these most joyful tidings, to whom he will and at what time he pleaseth; by whose ministry men are called to repentance and faith in Christ crucified..." (I/3). Those who receive the gospel "and embrace Jesus the Savior by a true and living faith, are by him delivered from the wrath of God, and from destruction, and have the gift of eternal life conferred upon them" (I/4). The Canons teach that the preaching of the gospel is the God-ordained means of the salvation of the elect in the fifth head, Article 14: "And as it hath pleased God, by the preaching of the gospel, to begin this work of grace in us, so he preserves, continues, and perfects it by the hearing and reading of his Word, by meditation thereon, and by the exhortations, threatenings, and promises thereof, as well as by the use of the sacraments."

In viewing preaching as "the means of grace," the Reformed faith reflects the teaching of the Scriptures. Article III of the first head of the Canons quotes Romans 10:14, 15, where the apostle says that faith is necessary for salvation, that hearing is necessary for faith, and that a preacher and preaching are necessary for hearing, that is, that the means by which God saves men is the preaching of the gospel. The gospel is the power of God unto salvation, and this is why Paul was not ashamed of it but was ready to preach the gospel everywhere (Rom. 1:15, 16). It pleases God to save those who believe by the foolishness of preaching (I Cor. 1:21). The decree of election unto salvation includes that the means unto salvation shall be "belief of the truth," to which the elect are called by God "by our gospel" (II Thess. 2:13, 14). The history of the book of Acts makes plain that it is the preaching of the gospel that saves men in the sense that guilty, disobedient unbelievers become forgiven, obedient believers (Acts 2:6-41; 3:12-4:4; 4:12; 10:34-48; 11:19-21; 13:38-52; etc).

Many passages of Scripture teach that it is the preaching of the gospel that saves men in the sense that the reborn, believing people of God are preserved and built up. Acts 14:21, 22 indicates that, just as preaching is necessary for the conversion of sinners, so is it necessary for the confirming of saints: "They (the apostles) returned ... confirming the souls of the disciples, and exhorting them to continue in the faith...." In Acts 20:28, Paul charged the Ephesian elders to "feed the church of God," that is, with the Word. In bidding farewell to these elders and to the church of Ephesus, Paul commended them "to the word of his grace, which is able to build you up..." (Acts 20:32). The burden of the pastoral letters of Timothy and Titus, addressed to pastors of established churches, is: "Preach the Word" (II Tim. 4:2) and "speak thou the things which become sound doctrine" (Titus 2:1). By this preaching, the saints are perfected (II Tim. 3:17) and recovered if they stray (II Tim. 2:24-26).

The second principle, therefore, that undergirds the Reformed doctrine and practice of preaching, both in missions and in the pastoral care of the churches, is that God uses the preaching to gather and preserve those whom He has ordained unto eternal life. There are elect, but they must be saved, and they are saved by preaching. Now this is ample reason to impel the church and preachers to preach the Word in season and out of season, within the congregation and without. There is no need of any notion of a universal grace of God to be trumped up in order to stir up our missionary zeal. Hence, in the preamble of the "Constitution of the Mission Committee," the Protestant Reformed Churches confess: "The Protestant Reformed Churches believe that, in obedience to the command of Christ, the King of the church, to preach the blessed Gospel to all creatures, baptizing, and teaching them to observe all things which Christ has commanded, it is the explicit duty and sacred privilege of said churches to carry out this calling according to the measure of our God-given ability. We believe that this missionary activity includes the work of church extension, and church reformation, as well as the task of carrying out the Gospel to the unchurched and heathen...."[5]

The message that is preached is the gospel, the good news of God's grace in Jesus Christ, the "most joyful tidings" as the Canons of Dordt refer to it (I/3). The content of the preaching is Christ and Him crucified. This is true, not only because the preacher preaches on the subject of Christ but also because Christ is really present in the preaching. Christ is "evidently set forth" in the preaching as the crucified one before the eyes of every one to whom the gospel comes (Gal. 3:1). A Reformed man not only believes a "real presence" in the sacrament of the Lord's Supper, but also a "real presence" in the preaching.

This message, though centrally the message of Christ, His death, and His resurrection, is as broad as the whole of the Scriptures. A Reformed preacher does not go to the unconverted with the poverty-stricken, false message of four spiritual laws that he has memorized and now recites, or with a little "gospel on a thumbnail" in which he was drilled for six weeks in a Bible school. He goes out with the Scriptures, all of the Scriptures, and he uses all of the Scriptures also. At one time, he explains all of Old Testament history and prophecy, declaring and proving that the Messiah of the Old Testament is Jesus (Acts 17:1-3). At another time, the approach and burden of his message is the power and glory of the one,

5. "Constitution of the Mission Committee," in *The Church Order of the Protestant Reformed Churches*, p. 43.

true God, His transcendence, self-sufficiency, spirituality, creation of the world, and providence, leading, of course, to the death and resurrection of Jesus (Acts 17:18, 22-31). On still another occasion, he may emphasize "righteousness, temperance, and judgment to come" as part of the "faith in Christ" (Acts 24:24, 25).

Nevertheless, we may specify certain basic elements of the message preached to the unconverted. First, the Reformed preacher preaches the greatness of the sin and misery of those to whom he is speaking. This is the judgment of the gospel upon man. The gospel declares every man to be totally depraved in his very nature, corrupt in all his ways, and liable to damnation (Rom. 3:9-19). It does this by proclaiming the holy and righteous God, Whose law all have transgressed and Whose wrath is revealed from heaven against all ungodliness and unrighteousness of men (Rom. 1:1-3:20). A Reformed preacher does *not* proclaim that the need of the audience is their unhappiness, lack of success in life, and earthly problems. Neither does he preach that there is in them any good or any ability for good.

Second, the Reformed preacher proclaims Jesus Christ as the only Savior from sin. He explains Who Jesus is, the eternal Son of God in our flesh, and what His work is, redemption from sin by the blood of atonement. He makes plain that salvation is in the risen Jesus alone (Acts 4:12) and that the only way to have that salvation, beginning with the forgiveness of sin, is the way of faith in Him (Acts 10:42, 43; 13:38, 39). As he proclaims Jesus Christ, he declares Him to be the Gift of God and the amazing revelation of God's love and grace (John 3:16). A Reformed preacher does *not* proclaim that sinners can save themselves, should cooperate in their salvation, or must do something as a condition upon which salvation depends.

Third, the Reformed preacher declares the promise that whosoever believes in Christ crucified shall not perish but have everlasting life (Canons, II/5). At the same time, he calls every one in his audience to repent of his sins and to believe in Jesus Christ, that is, he tells them: "Repent and believe, every one of you!" He also gives a warning that those who despise Christ by unbelief will be punished (Acts 13:40, 41). Those who receive the gospel and embrace Jesus the Savior by a true and living faith are thus comforted by the truth of God's love for them, Christ's death for them, and their everlasting salvation, that is, they are "delivered from the wrath of God, and from destruction, and have the gift of eternal life conferred upon them" (Canons, I/4). They are baptized and exhorted to walk worthy of their calling in the holiness of gratitude for God's gracious salvation.

This is a sketch, admittedly very brief, of mission-preaching, preaching to unconverted heathens, which is neither based on nor proceeds by a well-meant offer of the gospel. In fact, it is a sketch of missions from which the doctrine and practice of a free offer are rigorously excluded. There is no universal love and grace of God in it or behind it; there is no desire of God to save all hearers, either stated or implied; there is no offer of salvation dependent upon the sinner's free will.

But what is lacking for energetic, lively, unfettered gospel-preaching to anyone and everyone? If we Reformed churches can preach this message in this way, and if we are driven by the love of God for His sheep scattered abroad, what in our message or our approach hinders missions or evangelism? What are we unable to preach that should be preached? What can we not do that should be done? Where can we not go that the gospel should go? The sketch of Reformed preaching to the unbelieving given above ought to be familiar to every Christian, and certainly to every Reformed man, for it is nothing other than the outline of the message and approach of the apostles in the Book of Acts, made with an eye on the Heidelberg Catechism and the Canons of Dordt.

It is especially the call to repent and believe that is crucial, both as regards our controversy with the Baptist hyper-Calvinists and as regards our controversy with the well-meant offer. The former deny that there is, or may be, a call to all hearers; the latter subtly changes a summons into an offer. We must, therefore, look closely at the call of the gospel.

The entire message of the gospel is God's call of His elect in the audience. Through the preached Word, God efficaciously draws to Jesus all those whom He eternally gave to Jesus in the decree of election (John 6:37, 44); by the sermon, the Holy Spirit works faith in the hearts of those who were ordained to eternal life (Acts 13:48). Not just one aspect of the Word, e.g., the command "Believe," but the whole message is God's great "Come to Jesus Christ" to His people. When the preacher is proclaiming the most high majesty and righteousness of God, the Holy Spirit is working humility and awe in the elect sinner's heart. When the preacher is proclaiming the depravity and guilt of men, the Spirit is working heartfelt conviction of sin, pricking their hearts with sorrow and shame. When the preacher is setting forth Christ crucified as God's way out of the misery of sin, the Spirit is working knowledge of and trust in that Savior. When the preacher cries out, "Believe on Him," the Spirit irresistibly draws them, so that they come to the Savior. This is what the New Testament means when it states that the saints have been called (I Cor. 1:24); that they have been called by God through the gospel unto the obtaining of glory (II Thess. 2:14); that they have been called out of darkness into God's marvelous light (I Pet. 2:9); and that they are those who have been called by God Who quickeneth the dead and calleth those things which be not as though they were (Rom. 4:17).

Nevertheless, biblical, Reformed preaching includes the command to every hearer to repent and believe. This call is addressed not only to the elect, regenerated members of the audience, but also to the reprobate wicked. The preacher can and must say to everyone, "Believe on Christ." Nor is it merely the case that it is the human preacher who gives the call to all his hearers because, of course, he does not know who are elect and who are reprobate among his audience. When the preacher says, "Repent and believe," it is not merely the preacher and the sending church which call the sinners, but it is God Himself Who calls them. On the Day of Judgment, God will say to all those who rejected His preachers' call to believe on Christ: "Because I have called, and ye refused; I have stretched out my hand, and no man regarded; but ye have set at nought all my counsel, and would none of my reproof," therefore, now, "your fear cometh as desolation, and your destruction cometh as a whirlwind" (Prov. 1:24ff.).

That biblical, Reformed preaching includes the call to every hearer to repent and believe is plainly and emphatically the teaching of the Canons of Dordt. "The command to repent and believe ought to be declared and published to all nations and to all persons promiscuously and without distinction, to whom God out of his good pleasure sends the gospel" (II/5). There are "many who are called by the gospel (who) do not repent, nor believe in Christ, but perish in unbelief" (II/6). The Canons hold that it is God Who calls all those who hear the gospel and that His call is unfeigned, that is, serious: "As many as are called by the gospel are unfeignedly called.... It is not the fault of ... God, who calls men by the gospel ... that those who are called by the ministry of the word refuse to come and be converted..." (III, IV/8, 9).

This Reformed confession is thoroughly biblical on this point. The Scriptures teach that one element of the proclamation of the gospel is the demand of every hearer, "Repent! Believe!" and the Scriptures term this a "call." In addition, the Scriptures make clear that this summons is a *divine* summons, *God's* call. Jesus teaches this in the parable of the marriage of the king's son in Matthew 22:1-14. God sends out preachers to call to the salvation that He has prepared in Jesus Christ many persons, both Jews and Gentiles, who make light of that call and reject it. God's call through His servants is: "Come unto the marriage!" (v. 4), that is, "Believe on My crucified and risen Son, Jesus." The Lord Himself indicates the teaching of the parable to be that "many are called, but few are chosen" (v. 14). This verse exposes the error both of hyper-Calvinism and of the preaching of the well-meant offer. Against the former, it plainly teaches that God in the preaching of the gospel calls more men to believe in Christ than the elect, as many men, in fact, as the church finds on the highways of history. Against the latter, the advocates of the offer, the text plainly teaches that many of those who are called by the external call of the gospel are not elect, that is, that God does not call them out of any love or with any "sincere desire to save them."

Acts 17:30 states that "(God) now commandeth all men every where to repent." Passages such as Mark 16:16 and John 3:18, which warn of the terrible guilt of not believing on Jesus Christ, indicate that the gospel very really did call men who ultimately perish to believe in Christ and that it very really was their responsibility to do so. All of the Scriptures show that it was the practice of the prophets, of John the Baptist, of Jesus, and of the apostles to confront all their audience with the call to repent and believe.

As regards those who reject the call, the Canons and the Scriptures maintain that, even though they had not the least ability to heed the call, so that it was totally impossible for them to do what the call required — the impossibility of a dead man raising himself — they themselves are completely to blame for their refusal to believe. "The cause or guilt of this unbelief ... is no wise in God, but in man himself" (Canons, I/5). "It is not the fault of the gospel, nor of Christ offered (that is, set forth —DJE) therein, nor of God, who calls men by the gospel ... that those who are called ... refuse to come ... the fault lies in themselves" (Canons III, IV/9). It is their duty to believe. They know it to be their duty. God most earnestly and truly declares in the very Word that calls them that obedience to the command pleases Him, whereas disobedience angers Him (Canons, III, IV/8). The reason why they refuse to come is that they consciously, deliberately, wickedly, and foolishly hate Christ and life and love sin and death. Hence, God punishes them for this gross iniquity: "But when the king heard thereof, he was wroth: and he sent forth his armies, and destroyed those murderers, and burned up their city" (Matt. 22:7).

Since the gospel shows men the way of life and since it sets forth God's grace in Jesus Christ, those who reject the call are guilty of despising life and holding the grace of God in contempt. Advocates of the offer have sometimes argued that, without a grace of God for each man personally who comes under the preaching, justice cannot be done to the biblical teaching that those who spurn the gospel are guilty of the enormity of despising the grace of God. If this reasoning were correct, it would follow that without a "Christ for everyone" there can be no rejection of Christ; without a death of Christ for everyone, there can be no unbelief concerning that death; without a "sufficient grace" worked in the heart of everyone, there can be no opposition to the Holy Spirit; and without an election of all to salvation, there can be no despising of salvation. On such reasoning we are all compelled to become thorough-going Arminians in order to safeguard the reality of the wickedness of unbelievers. Never mind what is done to the glory of God, the worth and efficacy of the death of Christ, and the comfort of believers.

This reasoning is fallacious. Those who do not believe the gospel sin against the grace of God, not as if they resist and frustrate God's grace directed to them personally in an attempt to save them (the heresy of the well-meant offer) but in the sense that they say "no" to the Christ presented to them in the gospel. Objectively, they stand before Jesus Christ, the Revelation of the grace of God, just as in the Lord's Supper an unbeliever stands before the sign of the body and blood of the Lord Jesus, so that in their unbelief they are guilty of despising God's grace in Christ, just as the unworthy partaker at the Supper is guilty of the body and blood of the Lord, even though, as a matter of fact, that grace was never intended for them or extended to them. Theirs is a far, far greater guilt and punishment than that of the pagan who only holds under in unrighteousness the truth of God that is revealed in creation. Acts 13:46 ascribes such guilt to those who refused the apostles' call to believe: "It was necessary that the word of God should first have been spoken to you: but seeing ye put it from you, and judge yourselves unworthy of everlasting life, lo, we turn to the Gentiles." Similarly, Hebrews 10:29 charges

the apostate with the sin of treading under foot the Son
of God, counting the blood of the covenant with which
he was sanctified an unholy thing, and doing despite to
the Spirit of grace. So really is this guilt theirs that both
Christ and the apostles, as well as the Reformed preacher
today, are *angry* with those who refuse to believe (Mark
3:5; Acts 18:6).

It is clear then that the Reformed preacher, although
he repudiates the well-meant offer, can call sinners, any
sinner and all sinners, to repentance and faith and that
he can do this with all seriousness and urgency. Need-
less to say, he can do full justice to the tender, comforting
aspect of the call of the gospel that applies only to God's
elect, regenerated people, the call that is directed specifically to those who are broken and wounded with the
guilt of their sins (Is. 61:1); those who are consciously
sinners (Luke 5:32); those who labor and are heavy
laden (Matt. 11:28); those who, pricked in their hearts,
cry out, "Men and brethren, what shall we do?" (Acts
3:37); those who, on account of their sins, are thirsty for
righteousness (Is. 55:1) and willing to receive the water
of life (Rev. 22:17). Such regenerated but grieving
sinners, he tenderly directs to the Savior, saying, "Come,"
"Repent, and be baptized in the name of Jesus," "Take
of the water of life freely," "Believe," and promising
them remission of sins, rest, salvation, and eternal life
(Is. 55:2, 3; Matt. 11:28; Acts 3:38; 16:30, 31).

Indeed, the "offer-man" is unable to call sinners.
Inherent in the idea of the call is a lordly authority, the
authority of the Lord of lords, Jesus the Christ. An
"offer-man," if he is consistent, must *beg* sinners, and
this disgraceful practice abounds today. It is revolting
to anyone who has caught a glimpse of the majesty of
God, the excellent glory of the risen Jesus, and the
sovereignty of grace to hear the "offer-men" begging

recalcitrant sinners please to accept Jesus and come to the front. They conjure up the spectacle of the Baal prophets ranting and raving in their "altar call" for their powerless god to send the fire. Is it out of place for us to stand on the sidelines and urge these preachers to cry harder and longer because probably their god of salvation, namely, the free will of the sinner, is sleeping?

There is a command to all hearers to believe. But this "external call of the gospel" is not a well-meant offer. It is grace to God's elect who, as God calls them in the preaching, receive the gift of the Spirit's irresistible drawing in their hearts, so that they infallibly believe and are saved. To the others, the reprobate, neither is the call directed to them by God out of grace nor is it actually grace to them. Rather, it is God's righteous, serious declaration to them of their duty and His serious insistence that they perform their duty. The call makes known to them what they ought to do, not what God wills to do with them. Right after they have insisted that God unfeignedly calls all those who hear the gospel, the Canons deny that "God on his part shows himself ready to reveal Christ unto all men," as if God "applies to all sufficiently and efficiently the means necessary to conversion" (III, IV, Rejection of Errors/5).

God's purpose with the call to those whom He has not elected is not their salvation but their damnation. Hence, He does not give them the faith which He demands but rather hardens them by the preaching of the gospel. He has mercy on whom He will have mercy, and whom He wills, He hardeneth (Rom. 9:18). In every age, the elect obtain salvation, and the rest are blinded (Rom. 11:7).

There are several things that will not be found in Reformed preaching to the unconverted. Reformed preaching will not approach the audience with the declaration: "God loves all of you, and Christ died for all of you." It will not say to every man: "God loves you and has a wonderful plan for your life." It will not proclaim to all hearers: "God is gracious to all of you and sincerely desires your salvation." This message is a lie. Not only are these statements false, but they are also the bane of effective missions. Never did the apostles take this approach or proclaim this message to the unconverted. Such a message is incipient universalism, which assures the sinner that all is well with him in his sin — God loves him, and Christ died for him! — so that there is really no need for him to repent and believe. Arminianism, which blusters of its concern to save the lost, peters out in universalism, which blesses all religions, as well as the irreligious, and sees no need of any preaching of the gospel. Biblical preaching assures the sinner of God's love for him personally only in the way of his faith in Christ crucified.

To the objection that has been made that if the preacher cannot say to every sinner, "Christ died for you," he cannot command him to believe anything, the answer is simple: a preacher does not call a man to believe some *thing*, but he calls him to believe on Some*one*. He presents Christ and calls the hearers to believe on that Christ.

Second, Reformed preaching to the unconverted will never tell the audience that their salvation depends upon their free will, decision for Christ, acceptance of the offered salvation, opening their heart to let Jesus come in, and the like. On the contrary, it will make unmistakably plain that their salvation does not depend, and cannot depend, upon them, not upon their willing and not upon their running (Rom. 9:16). For Reformed preaching proclaims the gospel of *grace*. To preach that salvation in the end depends on man's will is to preach another gospel than the gospel of Christ. One could as well preach that salvation has to be earned by the sinner's works of obedience to the law. Reformed preaching will make clear, especially today, that the believing which is called for is not a new, grand work of man meriting or effecting salvation, but the total renunciation of all of man's efforts and entirely the gift of God worked in the sinner by the Holy Spirit. It will loudly declare: "No man can come unto me, except it were given unto him of my Father" (John 6:65).

Finally, Reformed preaching, that is, biblical gospel-preaching, will not promise salvation to everybody. It will promiscuously publish the promise that whoever believes shall not perish but have everlasting life as the Canons teach (II/5). The preaching of the gospel is at its very heart the proclamation of the promise. But the promise itself is particular. It is addressed to the believer (John 3:16); to the willing (Rev. 22:17); to the one who labors and is heavy laden with the burden of the guilt of his sin (Matt. 11:28). The promise is for the elect alone. This is Paul's doctrine in Romans 9. The word of God promising salvation to Israel must not be thought to be without effect because so many Israelites perished (v. 6). For there were only some in that nation who were the "children of the promise" (v. 8), that is, persons to whom God gave the promise and persons brought to life spiritually by the promise. These were the elect (vv. 10ff.). Therefore, the Westminster Confession of Faith is correct when it limits the promise of the covenant of grace to God's elect: God "promise(s) to give unto all those that are ordained unto eternal life His Holy Spirit, to make them willing and able to believe" (7.3).

Thus, the promise is sure and certain. The elect believer can rely on it for time and eternity; faith clings to that sure promise (Rom. 4:19-21). A universal promise, that is, a promise made to every hearer, is at once a promise dependent for its efficacy upon the sinner and a promise that fails in multitudes of cases. Such a promise would be unworthy of God, of no value to those who perish, and a source of enormous doubt for the believer.

All of which is to say: Reformed preaching is untainted by the well-meant offer.

Chapter 4
Is Denial of the Well-Meant Offer Hyper-Calvinism?

The doctrinal issue involved in the question "Is denial of the well-meant offer hyper-Calvinism?" is precisely addressed and thoroughly explained by our Lord's teaching in the parable of the wedding of the king's son in Matthew 22:1-14. God calls many men, both Jews and Gentiles, to the salvation that He has prepared in the death and resurrection of His Son. Many of those who are called by the preaching of the gospel refuse to come: "And they would not come" (v. 3). Some do come to the marriage with the true faith that receives the wedding garment of the imputed righteousness of Christ. The reason for this twofold outcome of the call of God in the preaching of the gospel Jesus gives in the concluding verse of the parable: "For many are called, but few are chosen" (v. 14).

There is a call of God by the preaching of the gospel to many more persons than those who have been elected. This call, however, is sharply distinguished from the call that God gives to the elect. The parable thus warns against hyper-Calvinism on the one hand, which tries to restrict the call to the chosen, and against Arminianism on the other hand, which denies any distinction between the call to the elect and the call to the reprobate. The Reformed doctrine and practice of preaching, obedient to the instruction of Christ in the parable, is concerned to avoid error on either side.

Right understanding of the doctrinal issue concerning the call of the gospel involved in the question "Is denial of the well-meant offer hyper-Calvinism" demands some historical background. In the 1920s, controversy erupted in the Christian Reformed Church (CRC) over the doctrine of the grace of God — the common grace controversy. In adopting the doctrine of common grace, the CRC committed itself to the doctrine that God is gracious in the preaching of the gospel to all who hear. It denied that God is gracious in the gospel only to the elect. The preaching of the gospel is a general offer of grace to all. Several CR ministers dissented from this dogma that the preaching is a gracious offer to all, holding that the grace of God in the preaching is particular — for the elect only. The insistence by the CRC that these men subscribe to the doctrine of common grace and the subsequent discipline of them resulted in the formation of the Protestant Reformed Churches (PRC).

Because of their objection to the well-meant offer of the gospel, the PRC are widely regarded within the Reformed and Presbyterian community as hyper-Calvinists.

A similar controversy occurred in the Orthodox Presbyterian Church (OPC) in the 1940s. This controversy centered on the person and theology of the well-known philosopher and theologian Gordon H. Clark. Among the charges brought against Clark by the leading lights in the OPC was that of denying the free offer of the gospel. At that time, the OPC virtually adopted the view of the preaching of the gospel set forth in the report of John Murray and Ned B. Stonehouse presented to the Fifteenth General Assembly of the OPC in 1948. This view, like the doctrine adopted by the CRC, maintains that the gospel-call is a gracious offer on the part of God to every hearer. The report states that "the full and free offer of the gospel is a grace bestowed upon all."[1]

The doctrine of the CRC and of the OPC on the offer has been influential upon other Calvinist churches and thinkers.

The controversy over the nature of the call of the gospel is of more than passing, historical interest. It ought to be of concern to others besides those denominations that have been directly involved. This is evident from the issue itself: is God gracious in the gospel to all men without exception? Every Christian and every church that professes to believe the sovereign particularity of the grace of God as this particularity is confessed in the Five Points of Calvinism, or doctrines of grace, has an interest, indeed a stake, in the controversy over the well-meant offer.

It is not a minor, peripheral issue. It touches the very heart of the faith known as Calvinism. Benjamin B. Warfield claimed that "particularism in the processes of salvation becomes thus the mark of Calvinism. As supernaturalism is the mark of Christianity at large, and evangelicalism the mark of Protestantism, so particularism is the mark of Calvinism." "Denial of particularism," according to Warfield, is nothing less than "the denial of the immediacy of saving grace, that is, of evangelicalism, and of the supernaturalism of salvation, that is, of Christianity itself. It is logically the total rejection of Christianity."[2]

The well-meant offer is a denial of the particularism of grace in the process of salvation.

If it was possible to smother the issue with a blanket of silence in the past, this is no longer possible today.

---

1.   John Murray and Ned B. Stonehouse, *The Free Offer of the Gospel*, p. 27.
2.   Benjamin B. Warfield, *The Plan of Salvation* (Boonton, New Jersey: Simpson Publishing Company, 1989), pp. 89, 90.

The issue forces itself upon Reformed churches today inasmuch as appeal is made to the well-meant offer in order to challenge the traditional Reformed confession of the sovereign particularity of grace. This challenge arises from within the Reformed and Presbyterian churches. It takes dead aim especially at the doctrines of limited atonement and of (double) predestination, election and reprobation.

The Dutch Reformed theologian M.J. Arntzen has called attention to the fact that the notion of the well-meant offer has been a powerful means to undermine predestination in the preaching and confession of the Reformed Churches in the Netherlands (GKN).

> One of the most important arguments that men suppose can be brought against the classical doctrine of election is the following: If God has determined from eternity that not all are saved, then the preaching of the gospel is made powerless; it is a threat to the earnestness of the proclamation. Indeed, how can one then maintain that God earnestly offers grace to all?[3]

In a recent book on Scottish theology, M. Charles Bell shows that the conception of preaching as grace for all has been of decisive influence in introducing universal atonement into Scottish Presbyterianism. The thinking that has prevailed in Scottish Presbyterianism is that

> the gospel message of salvation in Christ cannot be offered to one for whom Christ did

---

3. Arntzen, *De Crisis*, pp. 50, 51. Cf. all of chapter 3, *"De uitverkiezing en de tweeerlei bestemming van de mens"* ("Election and the Twofold Destiny of Man"), pp. 43-64.

> not die. To insist upon the contrary is to raise questions concerning God's veracity, and to undermine faith and trust in God. Unless Christ died for all, there is no warrant for a universal offer of Christ in the gospel, and, thus, no basis for assurance of salvation.[4]

Reformed theologians in the United States, convinced that the Canons of Dordt are in error in their teachings of limited atonement and predestination, are arguing for a change in the church's theology on the basis of the well-meant offer. Both by public writing and by official appeal to the church assemblies for change of the church's creed, Reformed theologians are contending for universal atonement and for universal election as necessary implications of the well-meant offer.

In a series of articles that appeared in the religious periodical, the *Reformed Journal,* Harold Dekker forthrightly argued that the doctrine of the well-meant offer, adopted by the CRC in 1924, necessarily implies universal atonement. Dekker began the article "Redemptive Love and the Gospel Offer" by quoting the first point of common grace in which the CRC asserted that God's grace toward all men is expressed in the "general offer of the gospel": "The first of these three points cites the universal gospel offer, along with natural blessings, as evidence for a 'favorable attitude of God toward mankind in general and not only toward the elect.' "

Dekker pointed out the obvious truth that the offer of the gospel is "redemptive in character":

---

4. M. Charles Bell, *Calvin and Scottish Theology: The Doctrine of Assurance* (Edinburgh: The Handsel Press Ltd., 1985), p. 187.

> Consider the universal and sincere offer of
> the gospel.... Can one really say that the
> divine love expressed in the gospel, in the
> good news of God's redemptive acts in Jesus
> Christ, is a *non-redemptive* love? How can a
> love which offers redemption be described as
> non-redemptive in character? Does that really
> make sense? The alternatives seem clear:
> *either the love of God expressed in the invitation of
> the gospel is redemptive or it is non-redemptive.* It
> seems to me that if it is non-redemptive, the
> gospel offer has no real meaning.

Since the well-meant offer is grace or love for all men
and since the grace or love of the offer is necessarily
redemptive in character, God's redemptive love for all
men and Christ's death for all are "universal factors
inherent in the well-meant offer of the gospel."[5]

Joining in the discussion raised by Dekker's
affirmation of God's universal redemptive love and
Christ's universal death, James Daane declared that
Dekker was (legitimately) developing the theology of
the well-meant offer: "Today, forty years later, Profes-

---

5. Dekker, "Redemptive Love and the Gospel Offer," *Reformed Journal* 14 (January 1964), pp. 8-10. The series ran in the *Reformed Journal* from the issue of December 1962 to the issue of May-June 1964 and included the following articles: "God So Loved — All Men!" (December 1962); "God So Loved — All Men! (II)" (February 1963); "God's Love for Sinners — One or Two?" (March 1963); "The Constraint of Christ's Love" (December 1963); "Redemptive Love and the Gospel Offer" (January 1964); "Telling the Good News to All Men" (March 1964); and "Limited Atonement and Evangelism" (May-June 1964). In addition, the issue of September 1964 contained an important reply by Dekker to a letter concerning his doctrine of universal redemptive love and universal atonement.

sor Dekker is extending the theology of 1924, asserting
that God loves all men."[6]

Whereas Dekker concentrated on the implications of
the well-meant offer for the doctrine of the atonement of
Christ, Harry R. Boer has demonstrated that the well-
meant offer refutes the creedal Reformed doctrine of
predestination in the Canons of Dordt.

> Obviously, the decree of reprobation and the
> unfeigned call of the gospel do not so (that is,
> harmoniously — DJE) relate to each other at
> all. The true relationship between them can
> only be described as one of flat contradiction.
> There is much in the ways of God with us that
> transcends our understanding or that is yet to
> be revealed, but we are spared the absurdity
> of being deprived by decree of what is granted
> by gospel.

Boer's view of the "unfeigned call of the gospel" is that
it is grace to all hearers, expressive of a sincere desire of
God to save all. This is also the view of the CRC to whom
Boer was speaking. Boer and the CRC agree in their
acceptance of the well-meant offer. On this view Boer's
argument is right and absolutely irrefutable: the well-
meant offer flatly contradicts the creedal doctrine of
reprobation and, thus, predestination as taught by the
Canons in its entirety.

Boer's conclusion follows:

> There is something that is terribly wrong with
> a divine predestination that turns the un-

---

6. James Daane, "From 1924 to 1964," *Reformed Journal* 14
(October 1964), p. 7.

> feigned invitation to faith and obedience into
> a formality that can never take hold of one
> whom God in his eternal decree has designated
> as reprobate.[7]

The well-meant offer is destroying the Reformed doctrines of sovereign grace. In light of this, those in the Reformed churches who love the truth of sovereign grace should re-examine the charge that the Protestant Reformed denial of the well-meant offer constitutes hyper-Calvinism.

In this chapter, I present a biblical, confessional, and historical defense of the rejection of the well-meant offer by the PRC. The biblical defense will base itself on Jesus' teaching concerning the call of the gospel in Matthew 22:1-14, the parable of the wedding of the king's son. Because the attack on the Protestant Reformed denial of the well-meant offer is three-pronged, alleging doctrinal, logical, and practical error, my defense will show that the rejection of the well-meant offer by the PRC is doctrinally, logically, and practically sound.

Let us begin by having clearly in mind the positions in this controversy over the preaching of the gospel. By the well-meant offer is meant the conception, or doctrine, of the preaching of the blessed gospel that holds

---

7. Harry R. Boer, *The Doctrine of Reprobation in the Christian Reformed Church* (Grand Rapids: Wm. B. Eerdmans Publishing Co., 1983), pp. 65-71. In 1977, Boer submitted "a gravamen against the Reformed doctrine of reprobation as taught notably in the Canons of Dort Chapter I, Article 6 and Chapter I, Article 15" to the synod of the Christian Reformed Church (see *1977 Acts of Synod*, Grand Rapids: Board of Publications of the Christian Reformed Church, 1977, pp. 665-679). Boer tells the story of the curious treatment by the CRC of this "gravamen," or objection against the creed, in his *The Doctrine of Reprobation*.

that God sends the gospel to all who hear out of an attitude of grace to them all and with the desire to save them all. The well-meant offer insists at the very least on these two notions: God is gracious in the preaching to all hearers, and God has a will, or sincere desire, for the salvation of every man who hears the gospel. In this chapter, the term "offer" will refer to this conception of the preaching of the gospel.

I deliberately refrain from describing the offer in terms of its implications. It has been charged against the offer by its foes that it necessarily implies both universal atonement and the freedom of the natural human will. Even though I firmly believe this to be the case and even though of late certain friends of the offer have been agreeing that the offer does indeed imply universal atonement, I do not here describe or criticize the offer with respect to its implications. One reason is that some advocates of the offer who reject these implications and deny that they are implications of the offer complain that attacking the offer in terms of these alleged implications is unfair. It is, in fact, attacking a straw man. Louis Berkhof, a father of the well-meant offer, made this complaint in his defense of the well-meant offer:

> Some men appear to be afflicted with the idea that this point (the first point of common grace adopted by the Christian Reformed Church in 1924 — DJE) contains the Arminian doctrine of a universal satisfaction (atonement) and, therefore, holds that Christ in reality has died for all sinners, head for head. To be sure, it is not supposed that the first point teaches that Christ effectually saves them all, but in this manner that He has opened wide the door for all and it now only depends on their personal choice whether they shall enter or

not. It is really perfectly plain to everyone
who can read the ordinary Dutch language
(Berkhof wrote in Dutch, and the "Three Points
of Common Grace" were originally written in
Dutch — DJE) that not even an appearance of
that doctrine is to be found in this point.... He
who alleges that the Synod is here attempting
to introduce the Arminian doctrine of
universal satisfaction in a deceptive manner
makes himself guilty of misrepresentation.[8]

Therefore, I rigorously restrict myself to that which
every advocate of the offer himself champions as sound,
Reformed truth and denial of which, according to the
advocate of the offer, brands a church with the ignominious mark of hyper-Calvinism: God's gracious
attitude toward all and a will of God for the salvation of
all in the gospel.

Just as the offer must be carefully and fairly described, so also must the denial of the offer by the PRC
be honestly treated. The PRC do not deny that the gospel
is to be preached to all men or that the preaching
includes a call to all hearers without exception to repent
and believe on Jesus Who is presented in the gospel or
that the promise of God that every one who does believe
shall be saved must be declared to all. But their rejection
of the offer is the denial that the preaching goes out to all
who hear from a gracious attitude of God towards them
all and with a will of God to save all. In short, these
churches deny that the preaching of the gospel is grace
to all who hear it. The basic question in the controversy

8.   Louis Berkhof, *De Drie Punten in Alle Deelen Gereformeerd
(The Three Points in All Parts Reformed)* (Grand Rapids: Wm. B.
Eerdmans Publishing Co., 1925), pp. 8, 9. The translation of the
Dutch is mine.

is this: is God in Jesus Christ gracious in the gospel to all who hear the preaching? The answer of the PRC is an unqualified, emphatic "no!" Neither is there a gracious operation of the Spirit of Christ upon the heart of the reprobate who hears the preaching, nor is there a gracious attitude in the Father of Jesus Christ toward the reprobate who comes under the preaching.

This opposition to the well-meant offer on account of the offer's doctrine of universal grace must be sharply distinguished, therefore, from the denial that the gospel must be preached to all men indiscriminately and from a refusal to call all who hear the gospel to repent and believe. Certain Baptists, especially in England, have limited the preaching of the gospel and the call of the gospel, "Believe on Jesus Christ!" to the regenerated. They have argued that preaching to all indiscriminately and calling all without exception to repent and believe would contradict the basic tenets of Calvinism, namely, limited atonement and total depravity.[9] This is not the position of the PRC. Nor may the position of the PRC be confused with this view.

Restriction of the preaching, particularly of the gospel-call, to those who give evidence of election by their regeneration is a real hyper-Calvinism. It is disobedience to the command that God gives the church in Matthew 22:9: "Go ye therefore into the highways, and as many as ye shall find, call to the marriage." It is exposed as erroneous by verse 14 of Matthew 22: "many are called, but few are chosen." The objection of the PRC to the offer is not at all that the offer requires that the gospel be preached to all, or that the offer insists that all be called to believe on Christ. But the objection is that

_____

9. See Chapter 1.

the offer holds that this preaching and calling are grace to all.

Denial of the offer by the PRC arises from a certain view of gospel-preaching. First, the church must preach the gospel to all people to whom God sends her, both within the congregation and on the mission field. This preaching consists of exposing the misery of all because of sin against the just and holy God; of proclaiming Jesus Christ as God's Way out of this misery; of calling all to come to Jesus; and of announcing the sure promise of God that whosoever believes shall be saved, as well as warning that every one who rejects Jesus abides under the wrath of God.

It should be noted that on the view of preaching held by the PRC the church does not proclaim a love of God for all, a death of Christ for all, a grace of God to all, a will of God for the salvation of all, or the promise of God to all.

Second, this indiscriminate preaching of the gospel is strictly controlled by and carries out the sovereign, eternal predestination of God, His election and reprobation. God makes the preaching of His church His powerful, indeed effectual, instrument of salvation for every elect in the audience by the secret operation of the Holy Spirit in the heart of the elect. God withholds the Holy Spirit from the reprobate in the audience (and, of course, church and preacher are altogether ignorant who they may be) in order that they not be converted by the preaching. Rather, He exposes their wickedness, renders them inexcusable, and hardens them in their sin, without infringing in the slightest upon their responsibility.

Accordingly, in the third place, denial of the offer makes a crucially important distinction between the call that comes in the preaching to God's elect and the call that comes to the non-elect, or reprobate. The calls are not the same. God does not call all men alike. God calls the elect through the preaching with the life-giving, converting, and irresistibly drawing Spirit in their hearts, whereas He calls the reprobate only with the external Word. He calls the elect out of grace, the grace with which He chose them in Christ before the foundation of the world, whereas He calls the reprobate in divine righteousness, requiring of them their duty, namely, repentance and faith. He calls the elect with the will to save them, whereas His will with the call of the reprobate is both their exposure as depraved rebels and the illustration of the sheer graciousness of His choice and saving calling of the elect.

The preaching of the gospel is grace only to the elect.

This doctrine is repudiated by Reformed and Presbyterian churches as hyper-Calvinism. It is not genuinely Reformed Christianity, but an aberration, if not a heresy. It goes beyond true Calvinism. It forces Calvinism to such an extreme that the result is a distortion, a caricature, of Calvinism. This position has overdone the sovereignty of God. It has overemphasized divine predestination, and it has done so in the crucial matter of the preaching of the gospel.

Denial of the offer is unreformed doctrinally.

Against this charge, our defense is, first, that the view of preaching that denies the offer is the Reformed tradition. This was the view of preaching of John Calvin. In his commentaries, in the *Institutes,* and in the powerful treatises that he wrote near the end of his life on providence and predestination, Calvin taught that the preaching of the gospel is controlled by the decree of predestination. Calvin also taught that the effectual, saving call of the elect is to be sharply distinguished from the outward preaching that comes to the reprobate unaccompanied by the internal work of the Spirit. Typical is what the Reformer wrote in the *Institutes,* treating the confirmation of election by the calling of God. His opening words are, "But that the subject may be more fully illustrated, we must treat both of the calling of the elect, and of the blinding and hardening of the ungodly." He continues, "The preaching of the gospel springs from the fountain of election." With reference to Jesus' words in Matthew 22:14, Calvin states, "There are two species of calling — for there is a universal call, by which God through the external preaching of the word, invites all men alike, even those for whom He designs the call to be a savor of death, and the ground of a severer condemnation. Besides this there is a special call which ... God bestows on believers only...." Having asked the question "Why, then, while bestowing grace on the one, does He (God) pass by the other?" Calvin explains, "because (the one) was ordained to eternal life," whereas the other was a "vessel of wrath unto dishonor."[10]

The view of preaching that denies the well-meant offer is the classic Reformed position as described in Heinrich Heppe's authoritative volume on the Reformed tradition, *Reformed Dogmatics.* In chapter 20, Heppe gives the orthodox, Reformed teaching on "Calling." The saving "calling," writes Heppe, "is imparted only to the elect." Heppe stresses the sharp distinction that Reformed theology has made between the call of the elect ("the internal call") and the call of the reprobate ("the external call"): "So there must be a distinction between the external call and the internal call." Reflecting Reformed thought, Heppe then denies that God calls the non-elect with the purpose of saving them: "More-

10. Calvin, *Institutes,* 3.24.

over outward Church calling is not imparted to the non-elect in such wise that God wished to present them with faith.... Otherwise the possibility would arise of a counsel of God being perhaps rendered futile by man...."[11]

This was a prominent view of preaching in the Dutch Reformed tradition that came down from the Secession *(Afscheiding)* of 1834 in the Netherlands. Professor C. Veenhof has pointed this out in his book *Prediking en uitverkiezing (Preaching and Election).* Veenhof acknowledges that a very prominent theology in this tradition, if not the dominant theology, was that which denied the well-meant offer and held preaching and sacraments to be grace only for the elect. This was the view held by the best theologian of the Secession, Simon VanVelzen. What makes this admission all the more significant is that Veenhof himself, a theologian of the "Liberated" Reformed Churches, does not favor such a doctrine of preaching. He explains its presence in the churches of the Secession as the carry-over of "scholasticism" into these churches.

One group of preachers in the churches of the Secession held a view of preaching that saw it as grace for every hearer — a well-meant offer. J.R. Kreulen was representative. In the preaching of the gospel, wrote Kreulen in 1857, there takes place

> the well-meant offer of the grace of God in Christ (Dutch: *de Welmeenende Aanbieding van de genade Gods in Christus)* to all who live under the gospel, with the purpose that they all would accept and obtain possession of that

---

11. Heinrich Heppe, *Reformed Dogmatics* (London: George Allen & Unwin LTD, 1950), pp. 510-542.

salvation, only on the ground of that offer
which comes to them as sinners.

Kreulen made plain what he understood by the
"well-meant offer." By "offer" he meant the declaration
of God not only that it is pleasing to Him that all who are
called should come to Him but also "that He promises
to all to whom the gospel's doctrine of salvation is
preached, to bestow (on them) grace and salvation."

This offer is called "well-meant," explained Kreulen,
in order to express that it is

> a declaration made by the truthful and holy
> God and that He earnestly, truthfully, and
> well-meaningly goes out offering His grace in
> Christ to all who live under the preaching of
> the gospel, without deceit, insincerity, and
> dissembling.

This is exactly the well-meant offer that reigns in
Reformed and Presbyterian churches today.

But it did not go unopposed in the churches of the
Secession. Outstanding churchman and theologian
Simon VanVelzen opposed the well-meant offer of his
colleagues.

VanVelzen considered the issue to be of crucial
importance: "It is the great question upon which everything here depends, 'What does one understand by the
general offer?' "

He had no objection to the offer as the preaching of
Christ to all, as a call to all to repent and believe, as a
declaration that it is pleasing to God that all who are
called should come, and as an announcement of the
promise of rest and eternal life to all who come and
believe.

But VanVelzen did object to the understanding of the "general offer" as a gracious promise to all who hear the gospel, that is, he objected to the doctrine that the preaching is grace to all hearers.

> But if one adds to this, "and that He promises to all to whom the gospel's doctrine of salvation is preached, to bestow (on them) grace and salvation," then surely no one who has some little esteem for the Word of God can agree with such an opinion even in the slightest. What? God promises to all to whom the gospel's doctrine of salvation is preached, that He shall bestow (on them) grace and salvation? He would thus promise and not fulfill His promise, as we see the evidence in numberless persons who remain unconverted under the preaching. This opinion is denial of God's truth. Nothing more about this needs to be said.[12]

However one may explain it, the fact is that the denial of the offer has an honorable pedigree. With good right, it may claim to represent the Reformed tradition. Those who dismiss it out of hand as a novelty only show their own ignorance of the Reformed tradition.

Far more important for our defense is the appeal to

---

12. C. Veenhof, *Prediking en Uitverkiezing (Preaching and Election)* (Kampen: J.H. Kok, 1959), pp. 45-57. This chapter is entitled *"Strijd over de 'Welmeenende Aanbieding' "* ("Controversy over the 'Well-meant Offer' "). The quotations are my translation of the Dutch. In a lengthy footnote, Veenhof points out that this very same issue reappears in the history of the Protestant Reformed Churches (p. 311).

the creeds. The Reformed faith is a confessional religion. The creeds are authoritative.

It is not to be found in "The Three Forms of Unity" that God sends out the gospel in grace for every human without exception and with the sincere desire to save every child of Adam. But the doctrine that lies on the very face of the Canons of Dordt in particular (and the Canons, we remember, are only an explanation of the doctrine contained in the Catechism and in the Confession) is that God's will unto salvation and His grace are for the elect alone (I) and that this gracious will is realized by the effectual call of the gospel (III, IV/10). The entire, massive weight of the Canons comes down on the side of the denial of the offer and against the well-meant offer in its essential elements: a grace of God in Jesus towards every human, a will of God to save every human by Jesus, and preaching as an offer made in love and with the desire to save to every sinner without exception.

The only possible appeals to the Canons by the defenders of the offer are to the use of the term "offer" in III, IV/9 ("Christ offered therein," that is, in the gospel) and to the statement in the preceding article that all who are called by the gospel are "unfeignedly," that is, "seriously" called. The use of the term "offer" proves nothing for the well-meant offer, since the Latin word "offero" which the fathers of Dordt used, simply meant "set forth" or "present." No one denies that Jesus is presented in the gospel to all who hear the preaching. What must be proved is the new meaning that has been poured into "offer" by advocates of the well-meant offer, namely, that it expresses love for all and the will to save all. The appeal to the mere use of the word "offer" in the Canons for this is little short of desperate.

That God is serious in the external call to all who

hear, reprobate as well as elect, does not mean, or even imply, that He wishes all to be saved but rather means that He commands all to believe on Christ and that this command is in dead earnest. Coming to God by believing in Jesus is the solemn obligation of every man who hears the gospel. This pleases God. All those called to the marriage in Matthew 22 ought to have come. Those who refuse bring down on themselves the wrath of God for their refusal. Unbelief displeases God. God can be serious in commanding someone to do his duty, even though God has willed that he not obey the command and even though God uses the command itself to harden him in his disobedience. Think only of Jehovah's dealings with Pharaoh in Exodus 4 - 14, as explained by Paul in Romans 9:17-23.

The Westminster Confession of Faith is in full agreement with the Canons of Dordt in limiting the gracious call to the elect. Chapter 3 teaches that God's eternal and free will is that the elect, and the elect only, be effectually called to Christ. Chapter 5 teaches that God "withholdeth His grace, whereby they might have been enlightened," from the reprobate wicked so that "they harden themselves, even under those means which God useth for the softening of others." Thus, God accomplishes His purpose to "blind and harden" these persons. Chapter 10 strictly limits God's desire for the salvation of men to "those whom God hath predestinated unto life." To them alone is God gracious "by His Word and Spirit." The "others not elected" are only "called by the ministry of the Word" and "cannot be saved."

In the light of this overwhelming testimony of Westminster to the particularity of the will of God unto salvation and to the particularity of God's grace, precisely in the matter of the preaching of the gospel, for defenders of the well-meant offer to appeal to the mere mention of the word "offer" in Chapter 7, in support of their notion of a universal will of God unto salvation and of universal grace in the preaching borders on the ludicrous. There is indeed an exhibiting and presenting of Jesus to sinners as the source of life and salvation under the covenant of grace. The blessings of salvation in Christ are proclaimed as free gifts to every one who receives them by believing. This is the meaning of the phrase "He freely offereth unto sinners life and salvation by Jesus Christ...," and this is Reformed orthodoxy. That it is a mistake to discover in the phrase the teaching that God desires the salvation of all and extends to all His grace is evident from the words that immediately follow: "... and promising to give unto all those that are ordained unto life His Holy Spirit, to make them willing and able to believe." As God freely offers life and salvation under the covenant of grace, His purpose, will, and desire are to give life and salvation to the elect only. In the gospel, His promise is to the elect only. And by the gospel, which freely offers life to sinners, He gives (not only "presents," but also "conveys") grace to the elect, to make them believe.

It is a curious thing that professing Calvinists, zealous for the well-meant offer, hold up the phrase in the Westminster Confession, 7.3, "freely offereth" as though it were the very essence of Westminster's doctrine of the calling, indeed the only thing that Westminster has to say on the calling, while ignoring not only all that Westminster teaches elsewhere on the effectual call but also that which Westminster says about the particular promise in this very article.

If the Reformed tradition is weighty and the Reformed creeds are authoritative, the Scriptures are decisive in our defense of the denial of the offer. The Bible makes preaching dependent upon predestination, distinguishes between the call of the elect and the call of the others, and describes the preaching of the gospel as the effectual means of grace to the elect alone. This is the doctrine of the Chief Prophet and Great Evangelist himself in Matthew 22:1-14, which concludes with the words "For many are called, but few are chosen." There is a difference between the call of the many and the call of the few, a difference that explains why the many do not come to Christ, whereas the few do come. This difference is due to God's election of the few, in distinction from the many who do not come.

God indeed calls the many. By His preachers He says, "All of My salvation is prepared now in the death and resurrection of My Son Jesus: come, by believing on Him." But He does not call them according to election. Therefore, He does not call them out of grace. He does not call them with the will to save them. He does not call them in such a way that He draws them by the Holy Spirit.

The few, on the other hand, He does call out of love, with the will that they be saved, and by teaching them in their hearts concerning their own need and concerning the riches of the marriage-banquet. The reason for this effectual, saving call is election: the few were eternally chosen.

Denial of the well-meant offer is doctrinally sound.

It is an aspect of our defense of the denial of the well-meant offer that we take the offensive: we charge, in dead earnest, that the offer is the Arminian view of gospel-preaching.

The Arminians of the seventeenth century set forth their conception of preaching in their "Opinions," delivered to the Synod of Dordt in 1618. They said this about the preaching of the gospel:

1) In the preaching God confers, or is ready to

confer, grace to every man.

2) God is serious in calling every person who hears the gospel because He calls "with a sincere and completely unhypocritical intention and will to save."

3) God does not "call the reprobate to these ends: that he should the more harden them, or take away excuse ... or display their inability." These are not the purposes of God in calling the "reprobate," since for the Arminians God calls all alike to "these ends," namely, "that they should be converted, should believe, and should be saved."

4) In summary, God calls all alike out of grace and with the sincere desire, or will, to save.[13]

This doctrine of preaching was fundamental to the entire Arminian theology. To give the devil his due, the Arminians themselves forthrightly pointed this out in Article 9 of their confession "concerning the grace of God and the conversion of man":

> There is not in God a secret will which so contradicts the will of the same revealed in the Word that according to it (that is, the secret will) He does not will the conversion and salvation of the greatest part of those whom He seriously calls and invites by the Word of the Gospel and by His revealed will; and we do not here, as some say, acknowledge in God a holy simulation, or a double person.[14]

On the Arminian view of preaching, there cannot be a decree of predestination in God excluding any from

---

13. See *Crisis in the Reformed Churches,* ed. Peter Y. DeJong, pp. 226, 227.
14. Ibid., p. 227.

salvation. And if there is no decree of predestination, as confessed by Reformed orthodoxy, neither is there any of the other of the Five Points of Calvinism.

The PRC see the well-meant offer of professing Calvinists as identical with the Arminian doctrine of preaching in at least two basic respects: grace for all in the gospel of Christ and a divine will for the salvation of all. It is incontrovertible that the offer teaches — does not imply, but teaches — that God's grace in the preaching is resistible, *and resisted,* and that God's will for the salvation of sinners is frustrated. Many towards whom grace is directed in the preaching successfully refuse it, and many whom God desires to save perish.

Indeed, we ask the defender of the offer, "On this view why are some saved by the gospel, and others not?" The answer cannot be God's grace and God's will, for His grace and His will to save are the same both to those who are saved and to those who perish. The answer must be the will of the sinner, free will. The well-meant offer is forced to rewrite Matthew 22:14: "For many are called, but few choose."

A customary response by Reformed defenders of the offer to this attack on the offer has been the appeal to "mystery" and "paradox." How the offer harmonizes with predestination is a "sacred mystery," unknown and unknowable. Defenders of the offer condemn denial of the offer as unreformed logically, that is, they criticize the PR use of logic in theological thinking.

Presbyterian and Reformed churches that defend the offer necessarily hold that God is, at one and the same time, gracious to all men and gracious only to some men, and that God, at one and the same time, wills that a certain man be saved and wills that that man be damned. Predestination has them teaching the one thing and the offer has them teaching the other thing.

This, they admit, is seeming contradiction, a "paradox." This does not embarrass them, for Reformed, biblical truth (so they argue) is paradoxical, illogical, and "mysterious."

The contention of those who deny the offer is that the God of the Reformed doctrine of predestination cannot be gracious in the gospel to all and that the God Who has willed the salvation of some and the damnation of others cannot will to save all by the gospel. Particular grace in the gospel is in accord with the particular grace of predestination. The definite will of God for men's salvation in the gospel is in accord with His definite will in predestination and, for that matter, with His definite will in the limited atonement of our Savior. The truths of the Reformed faith are consistent, harmonious, and logical.

Upon this aspect of the denial of the offer falls severest condemnation by the Reformed community at large: "scholasticism!" "rationalism!" "too logical!" "hyper-Calvinism!"

The denial of the "well-meant offer" is unreformed, because it is theologically logical.

We have listened to the charge. We have considered it carefully. And we are constrained by the love of God's own truth to defend the denial of the offer against this charge.

We do not hold the view of the calling that we do because we think it logical but because we think it biblical and creedal. Nevertheless, we regard the rational, non-contradictory, logical character of the doctrine as evidence of its truthfulness, rather than as proof of its falsity. That the denial of the offer harmonizes not only with such doctrines as predestination, limited atonement, and efficacious grace but also with the Scriptures' teachings about God's sovereignty, the power of preaching, and the bondage of the natural human will does not render it suspect but rather commends it.

The truth of the Bible, Christianity, is rational, non-contradictory, and logical. The Triune God is rational, non-contradictory, and logical. For this is the nature of His revelation in the Scriptures, and this revelation makes Him known as He is. Jesus Christ is "the Word," according to John 1:1ff., literally, "the Logos" (whence our "logic," so that even lingistically "logical" does not have to hang its head in shame among Christians), "the logical, non-contradictory Word of God." Because Jesus is the logical Word, He can declare God to us humans (v. 18). If He were sheer paradox, an utterly illogical Word, a Jesus Whose word to us is "yes and no," we could know nothing of God, salvation, or heavenly reality, which is exactly the condition of much of the nominally Christian church today.

Biblical truth is propositional. To deny this one must repudiate the Bible as such. This propositional truth is capable of being understood by the mind enlightened by the Holy Spirit, which is to say that it is logical and non-contradictory. Paul argues by reasoning from premises to conclusions, a procedure based on the logical character of divine truth. John instructs by contrasting opposites, a procedure based on the non-contradictory character of divine truth. Every human instrument of the Author of the Scriptures teaches on the basis of the fact that a thing cannot both be and not be, or be true and false, in one and the same respect.

The truth of the Christian religion, although it exceeds human comprehension, does not mock our minds. Although Christianity is, finally, supra-rational, it is not irrational. Although it ends in our adoration of the God Whose judgments are unsearchable and Whose ways past finding out, Christianity does not end in our despairing of knowing anything at all about His judgments and ways.

In our view of the logical nature of truth, we have the whole, great weight of Christian tradition on our side. Read Augustine. Read especially Augustine's close argumentation in his anti-Pelagian writings. Listen to Luther say at Worms, "Unless I am convicted by Scripture *and plain reason* ... I cannot and will not recant...." Read the church's creeds, not only the Reformed creeds but also the ecumenical creeds. They are logical. Ominously, all are being discredited today as "philosophical" and "scholastic." Consider the Westminster Confession's view of the nature of biblical truth when it says in 1.6, "The whole counsel of God ... is either expressly set down in scripture, *or by good and necessary consequence may be deduced from scripture....*" Deduction of the counsel of God by good and necessary consequence is an absolute impossibility unless the Scriptures are logical.

Jesus is perfectly logical in Matthew 22:14 with regard to the matter at issue: the call of the gospel. First, the very fact that He *explains* the twofold effect of the call shows Jesus to be a logical thinker: "*For* many are called, but few are chosen." If truth is illogical, explanations are ruled out. Second, the explanation is the difference in the call itself, corresponding to God's differing purpose with the different objects of the call. The "few" He calls according to election whereas the "many" are called only outwardly without any divine love or will to save. This is a logical explanation.

Denial of the well-meant offer is logically sound.

It is part of our defense of the denial of the offer that we take the offensive against the offer. We charge that the offer involves a Calvinist in sheer contradiction. That God is gracious only to some in predestination but gracious to all in the gospel and that God wills only some to be saved in predestination but wills all to be saved by the gospel is flat, irreconcilable contradiction. It is not paradox but contradiction. I speak reverently: God Himself cannot reconcile these teachings. Nor is there any similarity between this contradiction and the truth of the Trinity, which surpasses our understanding. The truth of the Trinity is not contradictory, for it holds that God is one *in being* and three *in persons,* not, therefore, one and three in the very same respects.

There is no relief for the sheer contradiction in which the offer involves a Calvinist in the doctrine of "common grace," as though the grace of predestination were a different kind of grace from that revealed in the gospel. For the offer exactly teaches that the grace of God for all *is grace shown in the preaching of the gospel.* This grace is not some non-saving favor directed towards a prosperous earthly life, but saving grace, the grace of God in His dear Son, a grace that desires eternal salvation for all who hear the gospel. The offer proposes universal saving grace, precisely that which is denied by predestination.

Nor is there any relief from this absolute, intolerable contradiction in a distinction between God's hidden will and God's revealed will. This is attempted as some kind of explanation and mitigation of the contradiction: the desire to save all (of the offer) is God's revealed will; the will to save only some (of predestination) is His hidden will. But this effort to relieve the tension of the contradiction in which the offer involves Calvinists gets us nowhere. For one thing, the will of God to save only some, not all, is not hidden but revealed. It is found on every page of the Scriptures. It is Jesus' teaching in Matthew 22:14: God has eternally chosen only some ("few") to be saved in distinction from the others

("many"). For another thing, the distinction leaves us
right where we were before the distinction was in-
vented: God has two, diametrically opposite, conflicting wills.[15]

Such teaching is destructive of truth and fatal to
knowledge of truth. Such teaching thrusts confusion
and strife into the very being of God: does God, or does
He not, desire every human to be saved? Is God, or is He
not, in His own being gracious in Jesus to every human?
I make bold to suggest that the god of the offer had a very
peculiar way of displaying his grace to all and of
carrying out his will to save all in the time of the old
covenant, when he showed his word unto Jacob but did
not deal so with any nation (Ps. 147:19, 20). Is it
presumptuous humbly to request of the offer-god wor-
shiped by professing Calvinists that he make up his
mind between the alternatives of the offer (the will to
save all) and of predestination (the will to damn some)?

Fact is, this contradiction cannot and will not be
maintained in Presbyterian and Reformed churches.
The one teaching must drive the other out. The doctrine
of the well-meant offer will drive out the doctrine of
predestination. Universal grace is intolerant of particular grace. The Arminians pointed this out at the very

---

15. This illicit and impossible distinction between two, opposite
wills in God must not be confused with a distinction in the will of
God that is taught by the Scriptures and sanctioned by Reformed
tradition: the distinction between the will of God's decree (God's
plan, or counsel) and the will of God's command. There is no
contradiction between these, for God's decree is His decision as to
what He will do, whereas His command sets before a man what he
ought to do. From God's command, e.g., "Let My people go," it
cannot be inferred that it is God's decree that the command shall
be obeyed, e.g., that Pharaoh will let the people go. See Chapter
7.

beginning of the effort to introduce universal grace into the Reformed church. Affirming in Article 9 of their "Opinions" that God's revealed will is the salvation of all, they denied any hidden will in God that contradicts this revealed will by decreeing the salvation of the elect only.

Evidence abounds in Reformed churches today that predestination and the offer are incompatible and that embrace of the offer results in repudiation of the theology of predestination. Official decisions are made by Reformed churches in the Netherlands rejecting the double predestination of the Canons of Dordt as "scholasticism" and "determinism." Synods of Reformed churches in the United States approve the boldest teaching of universal atonement and the sharpest attack on the doctrine of an eternal decree of sovereign reprobation. The most effective rejection of predestination, however, goes on in the preaching and teaching in the congregations and in the churches' work of evangelism. The prevailing message in Reformed pulpits, catechism classes, seminaries, and mission fields is that of a love of God for all, of a death of Christ for all, and of the ardent desire of God to save all. This explains why Reformed churches can cooperate in evangelism with the most notorious free will preachers and organizations. Of reprobation, nothing is heard. Of an election that constitutes one eternal decree with reprobation, nothing is heard. And this means that nothing is heard of Reformed, biblical election. But if nothing is heard of biblical election, silence falls over the doctrines of grace.

Indeed, it is now the rule that Reformed and Presbyterian theologians defend the universalism of the offer by appeal to those texts of Scripture that Pelagius used against Augustine, that Erasmus used against Luther, that Pighius and Bolsec used against Calvin, and that the

Arminians used against the Synod of Dordt: Ezekiel 33;11; John 3:16; I Timothy 2:4; II Peter 3:9b. The point is not so much that the defenders of the offer are found in the company of the conditional universalists of all ages, using select texts against the doctrine of unconditional particularism, as it is that their appeal to these texts on behalf of the offer and against predestination necessarily involves them in a thorough-going semi-Pelagianism. Their deep attachment to the semi-Pelagian doctrine of universal, conditional grace, despite their avowals of Calvinism, manifests itself in their hostility towards those whose only offense is their faithful confession of the sovereign, particular grace of predestination. They inveigh against these Reformed saints at every opportunity as "harsh hyper-Calvinists."

But denial of the well-meant offer destroys good, urgent gospel-preaching. Especially does it make evangelism and missions impossible. Denial of the offer is unreformed *practically*. This is a third charge of the friends of the offer against the denial of the offer by the PRC.

The charge is that a Reformed church that denies the offer cannot preach the gospel to all, cannot call all to believe, cannot do missions. Such a church has no compassion for lost sinners. She intends to preach only to the elect and can only preach to the elect.

This is a damning indictment. Any doctrine that restricts the preaching of the gospel in this way is false doctrine. Any doctrine that requires the preacher to ascertain the election of his audience before preaching to them is false doctrine. Any doctrine that binds the church to disobey the "great commission" (Matt. 28:18-20) and that forbids her to command all men everywhere to repent (Acts 17:30) is false doctrine. For God commands the church, "Go ye ... into the highways, and as many as ye shall find, call to the marriage" (Matt. 22:9).

But this is not the doctrine of the PRC in our denial of the offer. It is not intended to be our doctrine. It is not the implication of our doctrine. We have considered the charge that the denial of the offer is unreformed practically and testify before God and men that the charge is false.

Our denial of the offer involves no restriction upon the preaching, no rejection of missions, no embarrassment at calling sinners to Jesus Christ. We believe that the gospel is to be preached everywhere, to everyone "promiscuously and without distinction" (Canons of Dordt, II/5); that the ascended Christ sends the New Testament church out to do missions; and that all who hear the preaching are to be called to come to Christ.

The basis for this, however, is not universal grace and a universal will to salvation as the well-meant offer likes to have Calvinists believe. Rather, the basis is predestination. God has chosen certain persons unto salvation. These persons, found among all peoples in all places, must be gathered unto Christ by the gospel. For their sakes is the gospel preached to all. It is also God's will that the gospel come to the reprobate with whom His elect are mixed in natural life. It is not merely the case that the gospel unavoidably comes to them also because of their proximity to the elect. But this will of God that the gospel come also to the reprobate is not a will, or desire, that they be saved. For God has eternally rejected them, appointing them to stumble at the Word and perish (I Pet. 2:8). But they have an obligation to believe on Jesus Christ, even though they are unable to do so by virtue of their bound wills. And God wills to expose their outrageous wickedness, render them inexcusable, and harden them, as "vessels of wrath fitted to destruction" (Rom. 9:22), for His own glory and to illustrate the sheer graciousness of His effectual call to the elect.

All of this is to say that the necessity, the freedom, the promiscuousness, and the urgency of the preaching of the gospel are not *in spite of* election, but *because of* election.

We appeal to the teaching of our Savior in Matthew 22:1-14. Although only few are chosen, many must be called. This condemns all hyper-Calvinistic restriction of preaching to the elect or to the regenerated or to the "sensible sinner." Election in no wise hampers the promiscuous preaching or the serious call to all. But neither may the call of the many ignore or conflict with or destroy the election of the few. The sole saving purpose of God with the call of the many is the salvation of the few. The preaching of the gospel has its source, basis, and reason in the election of the church.

Denial of the well-meant offer is practically sound.

Having defended the denial of the offer against the unfounded and unjust charge that it restricts preaching, we may be permitted to put the hard question to those who criticize the denial of the offer as making missions impossible: do they really want to maintain that a faithful carrying out of Christ's command to the church to preach the gospel is impossible apart from universal grace and a universal will to salvation? This is what the defenders of the offer are really arguing here: good, urgent, promiscuous preaching, especially a serious call to every hearer, is impossible except on the basis of a love of God in Jesus Christ for every human and on the basis of a will of God for the salvation of all men. But this has always been the objection of Rome and of the Arminians to the Reformed doctrine of predestination and sovereign grace: the Reformed doctrine of particular grace, expressed especially in predestination, makes preaching impossible.

In Canon 17 of the section "On Justification" in its "Canons and Decrees of the Council of Trent," the Roman Catholic Church condemned the Reformation teaching that grace is limited to the elect *as a denial of the gospel call:*

> If any one saith that the grace of Justification is only attained to by those who are predestined unto life; but that all others who are called, are called indeed, but receive not grace, as being, by the divine power, predestined unto evil: Let him be anathema.[16]

The Arminians likewise condemned the Reformed doctrine of particular grace as a fatal weakening of the gospel-call in Articles 8-10 of their "Opinions" concerning the conversion of man. Article 9 has been quoted above. In Article 8 the Arminians gave their own view of the call of the gospel and rejected the Reformed conception:

> Whomever God calls to salvation, he calls seriously, that is, with a sincere and completely unhypocritical intention and will to save; nor do we assent to the opinion of those who hold that God calls certain ones externally whom He does not will to call internally, that is, as truly converted, even before the grace of calling has been rejected.

In Article 10 the Arminians repudiated the Reformed

---

16. Philip Schaff, *Creeds of Christendom* (New York: Harper & Brothers, 1877), 2:114.

doctrine that the call of the reprobate, though serious on God's part, is without grace for them, which is, of course, exactly the position of the PRC in their denial of the offer:

> Nor do we believe that God calls the reprobate, as they are called, to these ends: that he should the more harden them, or take away excuse, or punish them the more severely, or display their inability; nor, however, that they should be converted, should believe, and should be saved.[17]

Is it indeed true that the doctrines of predestination, limited atonement, and efficacious calling hinder, or even destroy, free preaching, urgent missions, and a serious gospel-call? Is it indeed the case that a Reformed church needs the teachings of universal grace and a universal will to salvation to come to the rescue, so that she is able to preach and to evangelize? Then Rome and the Arminians were right! Let us admit it! Let us renounce Dordt! Let us call a world-wide Reformed synod, preferably at Dordt, in order to rescind the condemnation of Arminianism and in order to make humble confession of our fathers' sins against Arminius, Episcopius, and the others! And let us come, caps in hand, to the head of Rome, acknowledging that at least with regard to its fundamental doctrine of sovereign, particular grace the Reformation was dead wrong!

While we are at it, let us also make the necessary correction in the teaching of Jesus in Matthew 22:1-14. As the explanation of the promiscuous preaching of the gospel and its twofold effect, let us put, "For many are

---

17. *Crisis in the Reformed Churches,* ed. Peter Y. DeJong, pp. 226, 227.

called and many are chosen, but only a few exercise their free will to accept the well-meant offer."

Thus, we will have arrived at the false gospel that Paul damns as "anti-gospel" in Romans 9:16: "It is not of him that willeth ... but of God that shows mercy." But we will, at least, be honest and forthright.

We warn the advocates of the offer that, so far is it from being true that the denial of the offer destroys gospel-preaching, the offer-doctrine itself corrupts biblical preaching. The teaching of the well-meant offer creates preaching that assures all and sundry of the love of God for them in the cross of Jesus. It creates preaching that then must proclaim faith not as God's free gift to whomever He wills but as the condition which the sinner must fulfill in order to make God's love effective. It creates preaching that soon adopts the most atrocious free will abominations on the mission field and in the congregations: the altar-call and all its accessories. It creates preaching that silences basic biblical truths, truths that Jesus Himself loudly preached in His own evangelism: "Ye must be born again"; "All that the Father giveth me shall come to me"; "No man can come to me, except the Father ... draw him"; "I thank thee, O Father, Lord of heaven and earth, because thou hast hid these things from the wise and prudent, and hast revealed them unto babes. Even so, Father: for so it seemed good in thy sight."[18] In the end, the offer silences preaching altogether, for more effective methods of winning all to Christ are discovered.

The well-meant offer is doctrinally heretical, logically absurd, and practically both unnecessary and disastrous.

---

18. John 3:7; 6:37; 6:44; Matt. 11:25, 26.

Denial of the offer, as this denial is found in the PRC, is historic, credal Calvinism.

It is simply the doctrine of the Lord Jesus: "Go ye ... and as many as ye shall find, call ... for many are called, but few are chosen" (Matt. 22:9, 14).

Chapter 5
The Historical Question

It has been our purpose so far to show that denial of the well-meant offer of the gospel is not hyper-Calvinism. Hyper-Calvinism we have defined as the error that denies that God's external call in the preaching of the gospel goes out to others than the elect and that inevitably results in the restriction and, finally, the loss of lively, promiscuous proclamation of the gospel. We found the essential evil of the well-meant offer to be its doctrine that God is gracious in the preaching of the gospel of Christ to all hearers, not only to the elect. Expressed as the teaching that God is favorable to all and sincerely desires the salvation of all, this doctrine of universal grace in the gospel is, in principle, the denial of election and reprobation, the denial of total depravity, the denial of limited atonement, and the denial of sovereign, efficacious grace. Opposition to the offer, therefore, neither stems from nor leads to hyper-Calvinism, but is grounded in the Reformed faith, or Calvinism, itself and is necessary for the maintenance of the Reformed faith.

Against the offer-theology we have contended that the preaching of the gospel with its call "Believe on Jesus Christ," which call is seriously made by God Himself, goes out both to elect and reprobate men, but that God's purpose with the sending of the preaching is exclusively the gathering and saving of the elect. The preaching is God's great dragnet cast out into the waters of mankind to catch the elect, and the elect only, from all nations, tongues, and tribes. In the preaching, God is favorable to the elect hearers only. His attitude of love and grace,

His sincere desire to save, is towards them only, and He gives the power of grace to them only. God's grace is particular; it is for the elect alone. As regards others who come under the preaching, God hates them, is justly angry with them, and purposes their judgment and condemnation through the preaching of the gospel.

Is our doctrine historic Calvinism? Is it the Reformed faith as this faith has developed in history? Or is the offer-theology the representative today of the Reformed faith in history, whereas our denial of the offer is a novelty, a recent speculation pasted onto the Reformed faith, and, therefore, to be dismissed as "hyper-Calvinism," or "ultra-Calvinism," or "high-Calvinism," or "hard-Calvinism"?

Advocates of the offer have clothed their doctrine in the impressive garb of Reformed antiquity. To change the figure, they have baptized the well-meant gospel offer as the legitimate offspring of the Reformed fathers, all the while scorning our denial of the offer as a bastard. In each of her "Three Points of Common Grace" the Christian Reformed Church ostentatiously wrapped herself in the flowing robes of classic Reformed thought by stating: "while it also appears from the citations made from Reformed writers of the most flourishing period of Reformed Theology that our Reformed writers from the past favored this view." Of late, certain Baptists have taken it upon themselves to give us instruction in the history of Reformed theology, alleging that Calvin, the Reformers, and the Reformed creeds teach the offer and charging that it is "the opposers of the historic Reformed position" who deny the offer.[1]

We intend now to take a look at "the historic Re-

---

1. Hulse, *The Free Offer*, pp. 9ff.

formed position." We will examine, not a few citations
snatched from here and there, but the body of Reformed
thought, as expressed in the Reformed creeds, as sharp-
ened in controversy, and as developed in certain of the
outstanding Reformed theologians including Calvin,
Turretin, and Abraham Kuyper. Let us see whether the
parentage of the well-meant offer is as honorable as is
claimed for it and whether it has a right to parade so
regally in the robes of historic Reformed Christianity.
Perhaps, after all, the offer is an ill-begotten progeny of
Pelagius, Rome, Erasmus, and Arminius in the Reformed family and the Protestant Reformed doctrine of
preaching as particular grace a genuine child of the
fathers.

Before we begin, several observations are in order.
First, the ultimate authority for the church's confession
and the ultimate criterion for judging doctrines is the
Holy Scriptures, not church councils and not the fathers
and their writings. This was Luther's response when his
opponent Erasmus appealed to the church fathers against
Luther's doctrine and pulled from the corpus of their
writings certain citations that favored Rome and contradicted the Reformation: "We hold that all spirits should
be proved in the sight of the church by the judgment of
Scripture." In asserting the sole authority of the Scriptures, Luther was not conceding that the fathers were in
fact altogether against him on the point in dispute, the
bondage of the will, for he claimed Augustine, the best
of all the fathers. But he was recognizing that the saints,
even the greatest, were weak, sinful flesh: "All that I say
of those saints of yours — ours, rather — is this: that,
since they differ among themselves, those should rather
have been followed who spoke best (that is, for grace
against 'free-will'), leaving aside those who through
weakness of the flesh testified of the flesh rather than of

the Spirit. So, too, in the case of those who are inconsistent, the places where they speak from the Spirit should have been picked out and held fast, and those where they savour of the flesh let go. This is the right course for the Christian reader.... But as it is we abandon our judgment and swallow everything indiscriminately; or else (what is more wretched still) we reject the better and acclaim the worse in one and the same author."[2]

Calvin's response to the charge that the church fathers opposed the Reformation was the same. In the prefatory address of his *Institutes* to King Francis, he denied the charge, calling it a "calumny." He thought that, "were the contest to be decided by such authority (to speak in the most moderate terms), the better part of the victory would be ours. While there is much that is admirable and wise in the writings of those Fathers, and while in some things it has fared with them as with ordinary men; these pious sons, forsooth, with the peculiar acuteness of intellect, and judgment, and soul, which belongs to them, adore only their slips and errors, while those things which are well said they either overlook, or disguise, or corrupt; so that it may be truly said their only care has been to gather dross among gold. Then, with dishonest clamour, they assail us as enemies and despisers of the Fathers. So far are we from despising them, that if this were the proper place, it would give us no trouble to support the greater part of the doctrines which we now hold by their suffrages." Nevertheless, Calvin insisted that the Scriptures must be the sole authority: "Still, in studying their writings, we have endeavoured to remember ... that all things are ours, to serve, not lord it over us, but that we are Christ's only,

---

2. Luther, *The Bondage of the Will*, pp. 109ff.

and must obey him in all things without exception. He who does not draw this distinction will not have any fixed principles in religion; for those holy men were ignorant of many things, are often opposed to each other, and are sometimes at variance with themselves."

The writings of the saints, including Luther and Calvin, must be judged by the clear, consistent, infallible Scriptures.

The Belgic Confession insists on this sole authority of the Scriptures as "the only rule of faith" in Article 7. This holds true for the doctrine of the well-meant offer. The decisive question is not "Do the Reformed fathers teach it?" much less "Are there now and then in the Reformed fathers' statements, inconsistent with the overwhelming thrust of their theology, which seem to favor the offer?" but the decisive question is "Do the Scriptures teach it?"

Second, there is place in the Reformed church for *development* of the truth. Because the Reformed faith is the truth of Scripture, the gospel, the living Word of God, the church does not only hand it on to the next generation unimpaired — although she may never do less! — but she also grows in her knowledge of the truth by the enlightenment of the gracious Spirit, so that there is ongoing development of the truth — richer, deeper, fuller knowledge and confession. That which lay implicit is made explicit; that which was hidden is made plain; that which was taught only in rudimentary beginning is carried through to its conclusion; a truth largely ignored is dealt with and given its proper place.

Nor is it impossible that foreign elements get mixed into the theological thinking of the church, which must then be purged, always by the fire of the testing Scriptures and always in accordance with the fundamental principles themselves of Reformed theology. Just think how foreign elements appeared in the apostolic churches: works-righteousness, gnosticism, antinomism. Just think how they were soon found in the church after the apostles: denial of the deity of Jesus, the innate goodness of man, the papacy. Just think how they were not absent from the amazing Luther: the physical presence of Jesus' body and blood in the Supper. Recall how the lie soon corrupted Lutheranism: synergism, which is nothing else than the free will doctrine which Luther condemned as the essential error of Rome. Even Calvin, who as an exegete and theologian towers over all others, does not escape. There are, e.g., in Calvin, statements regarding the extent of the atonement that not only suffer from lack of clarity but that are also erroneous, statements that are contradicted, to be sure, not only by the essence of Calvin's own theology but also by Calvin's explicit statements elsewhere, but statements, nevertheless, that head in the direction of universal atonement. Commenting on the phrase in Romans 5:18 "the free gift came unto all men to justification of life," Calvin says: "Paul makes grace common to all men, not because it in fact extends to all, but because it is offered to all. Although Christ suffered for the sins of the world, and is offered by the goodness of God without distinction to all men, yet not all receive Him." This exegesis is patently false for the apostle does not say that the free gift *attempts* to come to all men but *comes* to all men, so that all men actually *have* the justification of Christ's cross and *possess* eternal life. Calvin's error here rests upon his failure to see that "all men" in the phrase refers to all those represented by Christ, that is, the elect. The Reformed faith did not spring full-blown from the head of Calvin but develops.

Reformed preachers and theologians do not deliberately set about to concoct something new and different.

To teach and to hear some new thing is the lust of philosophers, heretics, and itching ears in the pews. But the servants of the Word labor with the Scriptures—real toil! They do this, praying earnestly and without ceasing for the Holy Spirit's guidance. They do this, gratefully receiving the theology of the church in the past, especially as contained in her confessions. The Reformed theologian *enters into* Reformed theology of the past. He knows it, wrestles with it, and makes it his own, and he allows himself to be guided in his work with the Scriptures by this theology. Thus, there is development of the truth, as naturally and inevitably as a seed sprouts, grows, blossoms, and flowers in rich, dark soil.

Herman Hoeksema has been instrumental in the development of the Reformed faith. The area of his outstanding contribution is the doctrine of the covenant: what the covenant is, the sovereignly gracious nature of the establishment and maintenance of the covenant, the inclusion of the children of believers in the covenant, the biblical basis of infant baptism, and related truths.[3]

The prominence of the doctrine of the covenant in the Scriptures and its significance for the Reformed faith are widely recognized.

The doctrine of the covenant is found in Calvin and the Reformed creeds, but in somewhat embryonic form. Through the years, Reformed theology has grappled with the question: what is the covenant? Sounder views and less sound views have been propounded. In time, a view of the covenant gained currency in Presbyterian

---

3.   For Hoeksema's conception of the covenant, see his *Reformed Dogmatics* (Grand Rapids: Reformed Free Publishing Association, 1966), pp. 152, 214-226, 285-336, 669-700; *The Triple Knowledge*, 2:504-553; and *Believers and their Seed* (Grand Rapids: Reformed Free Publishing Association, 1971).

and Reformed circles that jeopardized the sovereignty of God and the gospel of grace. It began to be accepted that the covenant is a pact entered into mutually by God and man, dependent on conditions fulfilled by both parties and serving as the means by which the covenant people acquire salvation. Notes in jarring discord with the sweet music of the Reformed faith began to be struck in the Reformed churches: a dependent God, the decisiveness of man's will in salvation, the extension of God's grace to a wider circle than the elect, the failure of this grace in many cases, and the achievement of final salvation through divine and human cooperation.

The better Reformed theologians heard the dissonance and manifested uneasiness with the covenant conception that passed for truth in the Reformed sphere. But it was Hoeksema who subjected that conception of the covenant to rigorous scrutiny in the light of the Scriptures; who rejected it, root and branch, as in fundamental conflict with the Reformed faith; and who, not without the aid of certain predecessors and some contemporaries, set forth in preaching and writing a "new" doctrine of the covenant. Hoeksema viewed the covenant as the living relationship of friendship between God and His people in Christ, as "unilaterally" established and maintained by God alone in free and sovereign grace, as a gift bestowed upon the elect in Christ and them only, and as itself the highest good for man both in time and eternity.

There are indications today that this view of the covenant represents real development of Reformed doctrine. One of these is the criticism in Reformed circles of the teaching of the "covenant of works." A factor that contributed to the development of the erroneous conception of the covenant as a conditional pact struck between God and men was the notion, popular

with Presbyterian and Reformed thinkers, that the relationship between God and Adam in Paradise was a
"covenant of works." According to this view, the
relationship between God and Adam was a legal compact between two contracting parties. The compact
consisted of a conditional promise as well as the threat
of a penalty. The promise was supposed to be the
promise of eternal life and glory; Adam's obedience to
the command not to eat of the tree of knowledge was
supposed to be the condition by which Adam would
obtain, even merit, higher life and greater glory; the
threatened penalty was death.

Such a view of the original relationship between God
and man led, naturally enough, to a similar presentation
of the relationship between God and men in Christ. The
essence of the covenant is still that it is a legal pact or
agreement between two contracting parties. The promise remains a conditional promise: God will save a man
on the condition that man will believe. Thus, man
himself continues to obtain, that is, merit, eternal life.
Although the new covenant was called "the covenant of
grace," it really continued to be a "covenant of works,"
the only difference being that the decisive work of man
upon which all depended is now man's *faith.*

One aspect of Hoeksema's repudiation of this conception of the covenant of grace was his rejection of the
covenant of works as the explanation of the relationship
between God and Adam in Paradise. That the relationship was a covenant Hoeksema strongly affirmed; that
it was a covenant of works he vehemently denied. Of
late, his rejection of the covenant of works idea has been
finding support among others. G.C. Berkouwer, who is
not noted for his praise of Hoeksema, has recently
questioned whether the notion of the "covenant of
works" has a rightful place in Reformed theology,

although he does not mention Hoeksema's longstanding and well-known opposition to that doctrine.[4]

Here and there men are also voicing dissatisfaction with the conception of the covenant as a mutual compact or agreement between God and men and are moving towards a doctrine of the covenant that approximates Hoeksema's bond of love and friendship. The Presbyterian theologian John Murray, in a work called *The Covenant of Grace,* has criticized the teaching that the idea of a mutual compact or agreement constitutes the essence of the divine covenant. Instead, Murray suggests that the covenant of grace is a "sovereign administration of grace and of promise." The essence of the covenant is "relationship with God in that which is the crown and goal of the whole process of religion, namely, union and communion with God...."[5]

The non-Reformed theologian Jakob Jocz writes along the same lines. Jocz has made a fresh, significant study of the biblical doctrine of the covenant. Even though the book is ravaged by unreformed teachings, including many concessions to higher criticism, it contains a doctrine of the covenant strikingly different from that embraced by many Reformed theologians in the past, namely, a conditional pact entered into mutually by God and men. Jocz asserts that the concept of the

4.   G.C. Berkouwer, *Sin* (Grand Rapids: Wm. B. Eerdmans Publishing Co., 1971), pp. 206ff. For the traditional view of the covenant of works, see Charles Hodge, *Systematic Theology* (Grand Rapids: Wm. B. Eerdmans Publishing Co., 1965), 2:117-122 and Louis Berkhof, *Systematic Theology* (Grand Rapids: Wm. B. Eerdmans Publishing Co., 1949), pp. 211-218. For Hoeksema's criticism of the covenant of works, see his *Reformed Dogmatics,* pp. 214-226.
5.   John Murray, *The Covenant of Grace* (London: The Tyndale Press, 1954), pp. 30ff.

covenant is so important that it is the "unifying principle" of the entire Bible. "Covenantal theology is at the
root of biblical thinking." He criticizes the notion that
the covenant is an agreement between God and men. In
close connection with this, he denies that the covenant
is conditional. Rather, the covenant is "the conditionless
and ... irrevocable will of God to be present to His
people." The "root-idea" of the covenant is made plain
in the tabernacle in Israel: "communion between the
Holy One and man," which is "the essential Old Testament message about God." Jocz argues that the covenant is unilateral. He quotes Weber with approval:
"the covenant in the Old Testament setting is 'essentially determined by one side' and ... it is God who acts
as initiator. It is therefore not a 'contract' in the usual
sense, 'implying two partners, but an arrangement
made solely by the one who determines it.' " He speaks
of "the one-sided nature of the covenant relationship"
and says that this is "decisive for a theological understanding of the Bible."[6]

I interject this little discussion of doctrinal development into our study of the call of the gospel for two
reasons. The first is that the teaching of the offer of the
gospel is bound up with the doctrine of the covenant as
a conditional pact between God and men. Wherever
men defend the offer, you will find them also defending
a conditional covenant, that is, a covenant depending on
man. Our repudiation of the offer must be considered
against the background of the doctrine of the covenant
developed by Hoeksema.

The relationship between the well-meant offer and

6. Jakob Jocz, *The Covenant* (Grand Rapids: Wm. B. Eerdmans
Publishing Co., 1968), pp. 9, 30-48.

the doctrine of the covenant, particularly as regards the covenant with the infants of believers, is generally recognized. Veenhof's account of the doctrinal controversy in the Reformed churches of the Secession makes plain that the issue of the nature of the preaching of the gospel was inextricably intertwined with the question whether the grace and promise of baptism are for all the physical children of believing parents or only for the elect among them. This involves the question whether the grace and promise of God are conditional, depending upon faith as a work of the children, or unconditional, depending upon the sovereignty of the gracious, promising God.

Also, it is striking that when Harold Dekker was defending his doctrines of God's universal redemptive love and Christ's universal atonement on the basis of the well-meant offer, he appealed to the covenant of God with the children of believers as an analogous truth:

> Perhaps an analogous question will shed some light on the question before us. Consider God's love in the covenant. Is it redemptive or non-redemptive? Surely it is redemptive. Is it not inherently a covenant of *grace*? Does not infant baptism express a love which must be described as redemptive? Or would some go so far as to say that the divine love expressed in the covenant of grace must be described as non-redemptive in so far as certain of its objects are not redeemed?[7]

But the main reason for this excursus is to point out

---

7.   Dekker, "Redemptive Love and the Gospel Offer," p. 9.

that an investigation of Reformed theology of the past such as we propose with regard to the teaching of the offer of the gospel must recognize the possibility not only of a lack of clarity on a certain doctrine but also of a lack of consistency. One must not be surprised to see contradictory elements struggling for supremacy, sometimes in the same godly man. So near does the life-and-death struggle of the truth and the lie come to us. The Spirit of Christ leads the church into all the truth, but only, as church history clearly shows, in the way of constant labor and battle. Examination of Reformed theology of the past, therefore, a going back to our sources, does not consist merely of compiling quotations from here and there. Satan, after all, can find quotations in the Scriptures themselves to buttress his case. As Luther said, we must discriminate when we study the fathers: "The places where they speak from the Spirit should (be) picked out and held fast, and those where they savor of the flesh let go."

There has been real development in Reformed theology as regards the doctrine of the covenant, and this development has included the Reformed faith's saying "no" to views that clamored to be accepted from within the Reformed churches and its purging of views which for a time even gained some acceptance. It is similar as regards the doctrine of the call of the gospel.

None of this should be understood as a tacit admission that Reformed theology of the past can be made to prove whatever one wants it to prove, specifically now as regards the offer of the gospel. The thrust of Reformed theology is perfectly clear, so clear that a child can perceive it. Its genius is plainly opposed to the theology of the well-meant offer. Reformed theology of the past, from Calvin on, stands up to say "amen" to the teaching that the preaching of the gospel is grace to the elect alone. It acknowledges this doctrine, as sharply and clearly formulated by Hoeksema, as its own well-born child and disowns the notion of the offer as illegitimate.

One other thing must be borne in mind as we turn to Reformed theology of past ages. We are concerned to discover whether Reformed theology teaches, or even favors, the doctrine that the preaching of the gospel expresses God's grace to all men, the doctrine that the preaching is motivated by a sincere desire in God to save all men, the doctrine that the success of grace depends upon the will of men, and the implied doctrine that Christ and His cross are for all men. This is what is meant by the well-meant gospel offer in Reformed circles today.

It is of no consequence, therefore, that the *term* "offer" appears in Calvin, in other Reformed theologians, and in such Reformed creeds as the Canons of Dordt and the Westminster Confession of Faith. The word "offer" had originally a sound meaning: "serious call," "presentation of Christ." We are fundamentally uninterested in warring over words. No, but we are interested to ask concerning the *doctrine* of the offer: is it Reformed?

Chapter 6
Calvin's Doctrine of the Call

John Calvin takes up the doctrine of the call of the gospel in book 3 of the *Institutes* in connection with the doctrine of God's eternal election. Where Calvin treats the call is significant. For Calvin, God's call in the preaching of the gospel is based on and controlled by eternal election.

In chapter 22, section 10, after he has taught that God elects some to salvation and reprobates others to perdition, he notes that "some object that God would be inconsistent with himself, in inviting all without distinction while he elects only a few. Thus, according to them, the universality of the promise destroys the distinction of special grace." He faces the question "How can election be harmonized with the call of the gospel to others besides those who are saved?" This question is really an objection to election. Those who raise it argue that since God calls everyone to repent and believe, there is no election.

Calvin's answer is that there is harmony between "the two things — viz. that by external preaching all are called to faith and repentance, and that yet the Spirit of faith and repentance is not given to all." Addressing himself to the assumption that the external call to everyone implies a universal grace of God to all and a universal promise to all, Calvin reminds such objectors to election that God is not "under a fixed obligation to call all equally." "He (God) destines the promises of salvation specially to the elect" (Is. 8:16). "Whence it is evident that the doctrine of salvation, which is said to be set apart for the sons of the Church only, is abused when it is represented as effectually available to all ... though the word of the gospel is addressed generally to all, yet the gift of faith is rare. Isaiah assigns the cause when he says, that the arm of the Lord is not revealed to all" (Is. 53:1).

The harmony between election and the call of the gospel to all who hear the preaching Calvin gives in chapter 24 of book 3. He begins by stating that he will now treat "both of the calling of the elect, and of the blinding and hardening of the ungodly." For Calvin "the preaching of the gospel springs from the fountain of election," that is, the preaching of the gospel is due to the eternal love of God's heart for the elect, is God's gift to the elect, and is intended to save the elect, and the elect only. Accordingly, the call of the gospel, "which consists not merely of the preaching of the word, but also of the illumination of the Spirit" is exclusively for the elect. God withholds the call from the reprobate.

Immediately, Calvin brings up Jesus' words in Matthew 22:14: "Many are called but few are chosen." Does this not contradict Calvin's teaching that God calls only the elect, and does this not indicate that God desires many more to be saved than only the elect? Not at all, says Calvin, for "there are two species of calling — there is a universal call, by which God, through the external preaching of the word, invites all men alike, even those for whom he designs the call to be a savour of death, and the ground of a severer condemnation. Besides this there is a special call which, for the most part, God bestows on believers only, when by the internal illumination of the Spirit he causes the word preached to take deep root in their hearts." The "special call," or efficacious call, which consists both of the preaching of the gospel and the "internal illumination of the Spirit," is for the elect alone. The call in the preaching comes also to many reprobates, but God's "design" with the call to them is that it be to them a savour of death and the ground of worse condemnation. Calvin does not regard the external call of the gospel as grace to all hearers or as an expression of God's sincere desire to save all.

Calvin comes back to the assertion that the preaching of the gospel, and particularly the call of the gospel, has a twofold effect and that this effect is determined by God's eternal purpose in election and reprobation. "As the Lord by the efficacy of his calling accomplishes towards his elect the salvation to which he had by his eternal counsel destined them, so he has judgments against the reprobate, by which he executes his counsel concerning them. Those, therefore, whom he has created for dishonour during life and destruction at death, that they may be vessels of wrath and examples of severity, in bringing to their doom, he at one time deprives of the means of hearing his word, at another by the preaching of it blinds and stupefies them the more." So far from being grace to the reprobate, the preaching of the gospel is a judgment against them, for by the preaching God blinds and stupefies them. "God sends his word to many whose blindness he is pleased to aggravate."

This is the teaching of the Holy Scriptures. God sent Moses to Pharaoh with His Word in order to harden Pharaoh's heart (Ex. 4:21). "But the prophecy of Isaiah presses still more closely; for he is thus commissioned by the Lord, 'Go and tell this people, Hear ye indeed, but understand not, and see ye indeed, but perceive not. Make the heart of this people fat, and make their ears heavy, and shut their eyes; lest they see with their eyes, and hear with their ears, and understand with their heart, and convert and be healed' (Is. 6:9, 10). Here he directs his voice to them, but it is that they may turn a deafer ear; he kindles a light, but it is that they may become more blind; he produces a doctrine, but it is that they may be more stupid; he employs a remedy, but it is that they may not be cured." After referring to John's explanation of this prophecy in John 12 that it was spoken of the Jews' inability to believe on Christ, Calvin declares it to be "incontrovertible, that to those whom God is not pleased to illumine, he delivers his doctrine wrapt up in enigmas, so that they may not profit by it, but be given over to greater blindness."

Calvin concludes his treatment of the doctrine of the call by considering certain texts appealed to by those who object to the teaching that God's call unto salvation is grounded in and determined by election. Strikingly, these texts are the same as those always appealed to by defenders of the offer and, as Calvin remarks in his "Treatise on the Eternal Predestination of God," the same as those appealed to by Pelagius against Augustine: Ezekiel 18:23; I Timothy 2:4; and Matthew 23:37.

Whether one agrees with Calvin's interpretation of these texts or not, it is clear that he does not explain them as teaching that God is gracious in the gospel to elect and reprobate alike or that God sincerely desires all men to be saved.

Calvin's remarks on Ezekiel 18:32 show this. The text reads: "Have I any pleasure at all that the wicked should die? saith the Lord God; and not that he should return from his ways, and live?" Calvin's opponents appeal to it as proof that God loves every man and in that love sincerely desires every man to be saved. Replies Calvin: "If we are to extend this to the whole human race, why are not the very many whose minds might be more easily bent to obey urged to repentance, rather than those who by his invitations become daily more and more hardened? Our Lord declares that the preaching of the gospel and miracles would have produced more fruit among the people of Nineveh and Sodom than in Judea (Matt. 13:23). How comes it, then that if God would have all to be saved, he does not open a door of repentance for the wretched, who would more readily have received grace? Hence we may see that the passage is violently wrested, if the will of God, which the prophet mentions, is opposed to his eternal counsel, by which he separated the elect from the reprobate." The "genuine meaning" of this much-abused text, says Calvin, is that "the prophet ... only means to give the hope of pardon to them who repent."

Calvin's doctrine of the call of the gospel is also on the foreground in his great work, "A Treatise on the Eternal Predestination of God."[1] Calvin wrote it, shortly before his death, against Albertus Pighius and Georgius the Sicilian, who denied predestination and affirmed free will. Pighius made grace common to all men in the offer of salvation, although it depended for its efficacy on the will of the sinner. Calvin calls this a "fiction": "The fiction of Pighius is puerile and absurd, when he interprets grace to be God's goodness in inviting all men to salvation, though all were lost in Adam. For Paul most clearly separates the *foreknown* from those on whom God deigned not to look in mercy.... He (Pighius) holds fast the fiction that grace is offered equally to all, but that it is ultimately rendered effectual by the will of man, just as each one is willing to receive it" (pp. 49-51).

Pighius, "this worthless fellow," thought to find an argument against election in the fact that "Christ, the Redeemer of the whole world, commanded the Gospel to be preached to all men, promiscuously, generally,

---

1.   Calvin, *Calvin's Calvinism*, pp. 25-206.

and without distinction." Calvin replies "that Christ was *so* ordained the Saviour of the whole world, as that He might save those that were given unto Him by the Father out of the whole world, that He might be the eternal life of them of whom He is the Head; that He might receive into a participation of all the 'blessings in Him' all those whom God adopted to Himself by His own unmerited good pleasure to be His heirs." The grace of Christ in the gospel is intended for and given to the elect only: "The virtue and benefits of Christ are extended unto, and belong to, none but the children of God." "If we see and acknowledge, therefore, the principle on which the doctrine of the Gospel offers salvation to all, the whole sacred matter is settled at once. That the Gospel is, in its nature, able to save all I by no means deny. But the great question lies here: Did the Lord by His eternal counsel *ordain* salvation for *all men?* It is quite manifest that all men, without difference or distinction, are *outwardly called* or invited to repentance and faith. It is equally evident that the same Mediator is set forth before all, as He who alone can reconcile them to the Father. But it is as fully well known that none of these things can be understood or perceived but by faith, in fulfillment of the apostle Paul's declaration that 'the Gospel is the power of God unto salvation to every one that believeth'; then what can it be to others but the 'savour of death unto death' as the same apostle elsewhere powerfully expresses himself" (pp. 93-95).

Calvin wants to "hold fast that the Gospel, which is, in its essential nature, 'a savour of life unto life,' and ought to be so to all that hear it, becomes 'a savour of death unto death in them that perish,' who thus remain in their darkness and unbelief *because* (Calvin's emphasis — DJE) 'the arm of the Lord' is not revealed to them" (pp. 97, 98).

Calvin makes plain that he is opposed not only to Pighius' doctrine of free will, but also to Pighius' doctrine that God wills all men to be saved, which two doctrines are ever and necessarily found together. *"Now let Pighius boast,"* writes Calvin, *"if he can, that God willeth all men to be saved!* The above arguments, founded on the Scriptures, prove that even the external preaching of the doctrine of salvation, which is very far inferior to the illumination of the Spirit, was not made of God common to *all men"* (p. 104).

Calvin castigates Pighius for teaching that the mercy of God extends to others than the elect: "After this, Pighius, like a wild beast escaped from his cage, rushes forth, bounding over all fences in his way, uttering such sentiments as these: 'The mercy of God is extended to every one, for God wishes all men to be saved; and for that end He stands and knocks at the door of our heart, desiring to enter' " (p. 152). By Calvin's standard, an accurate one, wild beasts abound today, running loose in even nominally Reformed churches. We will do our best to cage them and to muzzle their ravings about a grace of God for all that wishes all to be saved and that stands offering and begging at the door of the sinner's heart. Calvin refutes this "puerile dream" with the teaching of Romans 9 and Romans 11. God chose Jacob and rejected Esau before they were born or had done good or evil; God hardens whom He wills and has mercy on whom He wills; "the election obtained it, and the rest were blinded."

Similar is the refutation of Georgius the Sicilian. Georgius argued that the universal call to repentance and faith indicates that God willed all to be saved. For God to call a man to believe whom He had reprobated would be for God to mock that man. The form that this argument takes today is the contention that for God to

call one to believe towards whom God has no grace and
for whom God does not desire that he be saved would
be to deny the seriousness of the gospel call. Calvin's
reply is that the command of God to the reprobate to
repent is God's demand that they give God what they
owe Him: "For surely God doth men no injury whatever
when He demands nothing more of them than that
which they really owe Him...." Calvin readily grants
that the exhortations of the gospel are addressed both to
elect and reprobate, but he holds that God's purpose
with these exhortations is different in the case of the elect
and in the case of the reprobate. As regards the elect,
God intends that they "return to a right mind," that is,
be saved; as regards the reprobate, God's purpose is
"that lying stupefied in their iniquities, they might, by
such piercing appeals, be goaded into a sense of their
awful condition ... (and) prove themselves at length to
be incurable" (p. 174).

Calvin's doctrine of the call of the gospel, then, is
this. In the preaching of the gospel, God outwardly calls
all hearers to repent and believe, and the church must
call everyone indiscriminately also. God's purpose
with this call is determined by and is in harmony with
His eternal counsel of predestination, election, and
reprobation. He wills the call to save the elect, and He
wills the call to work the condemnation of the reprobate.
The call of the gospel to the elect is accompanied by the
internal enlightening of the Spirit, so that they are
efficaciously drawn to Christ by faith and are saved.
The call to the reprobate is God's demand, made in
perfect righteousness and in utmost seriousness, that
they do what is their duty to do. When God gives this
command, He withholds from them the Spirit Who
alone is able to give the repentance and faith called for,
Whom God is not obligated to give to anyone, and

instead hardens them in their unbelief.

We have now found for the defenders of the well-meant offer of the gospel the original hyper-Calvinist: John Calvin himself.

Chapter 7
Turretin's Doctrine
of the Will of God

We are examining the doctrine of the call of the gospel in Reformed theology of the past. We are concerned to discover whether Reformed theology has historically maintained the doctrine of the well-meant offer of the gospel, as is confidently asserted and widely accepted today, so that the denial of the offer must be regarded as conflicting with classic Reformed thought, if not as hyper-Calvinism. In the previous chapter, we looked at the theology of John Calvin. We now consider Francis Turretin.

Francis Turretin was a Reformed pastor and professor of theology in the seventeenth century. Born in 1623, only four years after the Synod of Dordt, he became professor of theology at Calvin's academy in Geneva, Switzerland, in 1652. He was a successor of Calvin, therefore, less than 100 years after Calvin's death and about 50 years after the death of Calvin's immediate successor, Theodore Beza. Turretin is universally acknowledged as a significant, faithful proponent and defender of the Reformed theology of Calvin and the Synod of Dordt. *The New Schaff-Herzog Encyclopedia of Religious Knowledge* describes him "as an earnest defender of the orthodoxy represented by the Synod of Dort,"[1] and Presbyterian theologian John H. Gerstner refers to him as "the greatest champion of the high-

---

1. *The New Schaff-Herzog Encyclopedia of Religious Knowledge*, ed. Samuel Macauley Jackson (New York and London: Funk and Wagnals Company, 1912), 12:43.

reformed orthodoxy of the seventeenth century."[2] The theology of Turretin, therefore, can safely be regarded as the expression of classic Reformed thought. What makes his theology even more significant is the fact that immediately after Turretin's death the Reformed Church in Geneva apostatized from the Reformed faith, ironically, through Turretin's own son, Jean Alphonse.

Turretin's theology is found in his three-volume work *Institutes of Elenctic Theology*. Turretin treats the doctrine of the call of the gospel in two sections of this work. The subject comes up first in the section on "The Decrees of God in General and Predestination in Particular."[3] After explaining and defending the Reformed doctrine of double predestination, Turretin investigates whether there is in God any will or purpose of having mercy upon all men and of saving all men, which will or purpose is reflected in the call of the gospel. The viewpoint here is that of God's will. The issue, in reality, is the teaching of the defenders of the offer that there is in God a sincere desire to save all men and their squaring of this "desire" with the decree of election by the positing of two wills in God, one will to save only the elect and another will to save everyone.

---

2.   In the preface of selections from George Musgrave Giger's translation of Turretin's *Institutio Theologiae Electicae* that Dr. Gerstner prepared and distributed for his classes at Pittsburgh Theological Seminary. Since at the time of this writing only the first volume of Turretin's three-volume work has been published in English translation, my quotations from that section of Turretin's dogmatics that treats "Vocation and Faith" in the latter part of this chapter are taken from the nearly 600-page volume of selections made available by Dr. Gerstner.
3.   Francis Turretin, *Institutes of Elenctic Theology*, ed. James T. Dennison, Jr., trans. George Musgrave Giger (Phillipsburg, New Jersey: P & R Publishing, 1992), 1:311-430.

Turretin heads his treatment of this issue with a question: "Can there be attributed to God any conditional will, or universal purpose of pitying the whole human race fallen in sin, of destinating Christ as Mediator to each and all, and of calling them all to a saving participation of his benefits?" His immediate, clear, and conclusive answer, on behalf of Reformed orthodoxy, is: "We deny." Such a view Turretin attributes to the Lutherans, the Arminians, and certain Reformed theologians who by "extending more widely the periphery of grace and defending the universality of mercy, redemption and calling ... depart from the doctrine thus far received in our churches" (p. 395).

First of all, Turretin explains the question. "The question is not whether there is in God a will commanding and approving faith and the salvation of men; nor whether God in the gospel commands men to believe and repent if they wish to be saved; nor whether it pleases him for me to believe and be saved. For no one denies that God is pleased with the conversion and life of the sinner rather than with his death.... But the question is whether from such a will approving and commanding what men must do in order to obtain salvation, can be gathered any will or purpose of God by which he intended the salvation of all and everyone under the condition of faith...." "The question may be reduced to these boundaries — whether there is in God a general decree; whether it is called a counsel or purpose or a conditional will by which God truly and earnestly intended to have mercy unto salvation upon each and every one (not by giving faith, but by sending Christ for each and every one and calling all to salvation under the condition of faith and repentance). The patrons of universal grace maintain this; we deny it" (p. 397).

Next, he proves that there is no such gracious will or purpose towards all men in God. The first proof is obtained "from the decree of election and reprobation. Because the Scripture makes the purpose of having mercy particular, not universal (since it testifies that God had mercy upon some certain persons only, loves them and inscribes them in the book of life, but hates, hardens, appoints to wrath, and ordains to condemnation others, Rom. 9:11, 12, 13, 18, 22; I Thess. 5:9; I Pet. 2:8). Who would say that God willed to pity unto salvation those whom he reprobated from eternity; and most seriously intended for them the end under a condition, whom by the same act of will he excluded from the means of ever arriving at that end? And who does not see that the conditional purpose to give salvation to innumerable persons is destroyed by the absolute purpose concerning the not giving of faith to them?"

Against this proof, it was objected that, in addition to the merciful will of God in election that effectually saves, there is also a merciful will that does not save, exactly the position of the present-day defenders of the offer. Turretin's reply to this objection is devastating: "It is gratuitously supposed that there is that twofold purpose of having mercy, while the Scripture draws every purpose of God's mercy from his eternal election; yea, it makes election itself to consist in it (Rom. 8:28, 29; 9:11; Eph. 1:11; 2 Tim. 1:9). And the thing itself teaches that it cannot be conceived without absurdity — that God (in whom there cannot be priority and posteriority, and who decrees all things by a sole and most simple act of will) by the same act willed most seriously to intend salvation for some under a certain condition; and at the same time, he (who alone can give) determined to deny to them the very condition without which salvation cannot be obtained. What else is this than to will to have mercy and not to will at the same time? I confess that the sole act of the divine will can be divided into various acts (which may be conceived as prior and posterior), but this is to be understood only of those which do not butt against each other and destroy themselves. Now to say that God intended salvation for all and at the same time decreed to elect and love some, but to hate and reprobate others, is most absurd. Nor can they at the same time stand with God (or even successively) unless his will is supposed to be liable to change (which is blasphemous)" (p. 399).

The second proof is that, if God earnestly willed the salvation of all men, He would also will all the means necessary to that end, e.g., the preaching of the gospel and the gift of faith, and would actually confer salvation upon all. But this, of course, is not the case. Turretin's argument here is that by the notion of a sincere, merciful desire to save all, "wants and vehement desires (yet fruitless and frustrated) are attributed to God by which he is made to intend and in earnest will that, which willing, he yet knew never would be or could be." This, says Turretin, is not "becoming to the majesty of the supreme deity"; is "repugnant to his wisdom and power"; obscures and lessens the divine goodness and grace, making God's goodness and grace "vain and inefficacious" (pp. 400-404).

In short, Turretin condemns the doctrine of a sincere desire of God to save all men as a denial both of God's sovereignty and of God's truthfulness. It is a denial of God's sovereignty because God's will to save is not realized; it is a denial of God's truthfulness because it represents God as desiring to save many whom He has no intention of saving.

In a fascinating section, Turretin turns his attention to several passages of Scripture that the opponents of

Reformed orthodoxy brought up (already in the seventeenth century!) in support of a divine desire or will to save all men. John 3:16 is the first passage. Turretin insists that "the love treated in John 3:16 ... cannot be universal towards each and every one, but special towards a few." It has reference "only (to) those chosen out of the world." As for the word *world*, "why then should 'the world' not be taken universally for individuals, but indefinitely for anyone (Jews as well as Gentiles, without distinction of nation, language and condition) that he may be said to have loved the human race inasmuch as he was unwilling to destroy it entirely, but decreed to save some certain person out of it; not only from one people as before, but from all indiscriminately although the effects of that love should not be extended to each individual, but only to some certain ones (viz., those chosen out of the world)? And nothing is more frequent in common conversation than to attribute to a community something with respect to some certain individual, not to all" (pp. 405-408).

Those who teach a sincere desire of God to save all always appeal to I Timothy 2:4: "Who (God) will have all men to be saved...." Turretin will have nothing of such an interpretation of this text. "The particle 'all' is taken here not distributively (for the individuals of classes), but collectively (for classes of individuals), that is, as Beza renders it 'for all sorts' ... from every nation, condition, age and sex. In this sense, God wills not that all men individually, but some from every class or order of men should be saved."

Against those who explain the text to mean that God sincerely desires every human to be saved, Turretin argues, "If God wills this, how does it happen that it is not done, since his will properly so called is always efficacious and accomplishes what he wills and which nothing can resist? Again, God wills them all to come to the knowledge of the truth either absolutely (and so all would come to it, which is false) or under a condition. But what can that be? If they hear it? But he does not have it preached to many. If they believe? But to believe is to have arrived already at the knowledge of the truth."

The truth of the matter, writes Turretin, is this: "God wills all those to be saved for whom Christ gave himself as a ransom *(antilytron)* (as their Mediator by substituting himself in their place and suffering in their stead the punishment due to them).... Now this cannot be said of each and every man in particular without by that very thing each and every man being actually saved (which no one would say)" (pp. 408-412).

As for II Peter 3:9, "The Lord ... is longsuffering to usward, not willing that any should perish, but that all should come to repentance," the will of God here spoken of "should not be extended further than to the elect and believers (for whose sake God puts off the consummation of ages until their number shall be completed." This is evident from "the pronoun 'us' (which precedes with sufficient clearness designating the elect and believers, as elsewhere more than once) and to explain which he adds 'not willing that any' (i.e., of us) 'should perish' " (p. 412).

Our Reformed theologian of this very flourishing period of Reformed theology then takes up the crucial issue of God's commanding all men, including the reprobate, to repent and believe. It is obvious that God does in the gospel command the reprobate to believe on Christ. Those who departed from Reformed orthodoxy in Turretin's day argued that this command indicated a gracious attitude on God's part towards the reprobate, a real desire of God that they be saved. Exactly this is the position of the defenders of the offer in our day. On the universal command to believe they base a sincere desire of God to save all men. They call this desire "God's revealed will" in distinction from "God's hidden will" (of predestination). These two diametrically opposed wills of God are then supposed to exist side by side in Reformed theology in paradoxical tension: God wills to save everybody, and God wills to save only some.

To this position Hoeksema referred when he spoke of the "double-track theology" of Reformed churches that championed the well-meant offer and when he spoke of the "Janus head" of such churches.[4] The advocates of the offer, on their part, denounce the rejection of the offer, that is, the rejection of a sincere desire of God to save all, made in the name of predestination, as an overly rigorous exercise of logic.

Turretin holds that the Scriptures do indeed teach a distinction in the will of God. The proper Biblical distinction is that between God's decretive will and God's preceptive will (the will of God's decree and the will of God's precept, or command). The former is God's eternal decree determining a man's destiny, e.g., that He will harden Pharaoh unto damnation; the latter is God's command to a man setting forth his duty, e..g., that Pharaoh must let God's people go. From God's command, one may not infer God's intention (sincere desire), for the command "Let My people go!" only indicates Pharaoh's duty and that freeing God's people, not keeping them in slavery, is pleasing to God. "Nor immediately does he (God) intend what is commanded, since many things are commanded which are by no

---

4. Janus was the Roman god with two faces looking in opposite directions. Reformed churches that hold the offer, charged Hoeksema, have two faces, an Arminian face of universal grace and a Calvinistic face of particular grace.

means intended. Thus God commanded Pharaoh to let the people go and yet he cannot be said to have actually intended (either absolutely or conditionally) their dismission since he intended on the contrary the hardening of Pharaoh and the retention of the people."

To explain God's universal demands of repentance and faith as indicative of a mercy of God for all and of a will of God to save all is to be guilty of ascribing to God two wills that "butt against each other and destroy themselves" and is to be guilty of adopting the Arminian denial of sovereign grace. "So from the command to believe and repent, you would notwithstanding falsely infer that God by that very thing intended the faith and repentance and so the salvation of all those, to whom such an external command is promulgated." "Therefore the precept signifies that God really wills to enjoin that upon us, but not that he really wills or intends that what is commanded should take place" (pp. 413-414).

It is evident from Turretin's theology that those in the Reformed camp today who defend the offer's teaching of a sincere, merciful desire in God to save everyone in terms of two contradictory wills in God have not a leg to stand on as far as historic Reformed theology is concerned. Reformed theology knows only of a distinction between the will of God's decree (election) and the will of God's command ("Repent and believe!"). Reformed theology has expressly denied that the latter implies God's mercy or will to save everyone to whom the command comes. It has condemned those who taught that the command to believe necessarily indicates a gracious purpose of saving in God. Reformed theology has always held that there is one gracious will in God which intends salvation for men: election. Therefore, there is not for Reformed theology any contradiction in the twofold will of God. God's command to Pharaoh, "Let My people go!" does not contradict God's decree, "I will harden Pharaoh's heart, so that he will not let My people go." For the command does not indicate God's purpose but Pharaoh's calling.

Indeed, although it is true here too that God's ways are higher than our ways and past finding out, there is harmony in God's twofold will. First, the command realizes and maintains that essential characteristic of God's decree that consists of the decree's being fulfilled only in the way of the full maintenance of the complete responsibility of man. Second, the command serves the effecting of the decree. By the Word of Jehovah, "Let My people go," the heart of Pharaoh is hardened by God, so that God can make His power known in that proud monarch.

So far Turretin has been touching on the truth of God's call to men in the gospel from the viewpoint of God's decree. He deals with the doctrine of the call directly in the section on "Vocation and Faith."[5] He defines vocation (the calling) as "an act of the grace of God in Christ, by which he calls men dead in sin and lost in Adam, by the preaching of the Gospel and the power of the Holy Spirit, to union with Christ and to the salvation to be obtained in him." It is apparent that Turretin views the call of the gospel as God's gracious, efficacious drawing of the elect. He states this explicitly: "All the elect, and they alone are called." Yet, Turretin recognizes that the Scriptures teach a calling by God in the preaching of the gospel of all who come under the preaching. Therefore, he distinguishes "a twofold voca-

---

5. The quotations that follow are taken from the selections from Turretin's *Institutes* distributed by John H. Gerstner. These are a faithful copy of the Giger translation (see footnote 2). The peculiar punctuation and use of capital letters are those of the original Giger manuscript.

tion ... viz., an external and internal. The former takes place only by the ministry of the word and sacrament.... The latter, however, with the additional internal and omnipotent power of the Holy Spirit." With the external calling, God calls also the reprobate; "knocks only at the ears of the body"; and "acts imperatively only, exacting from man duty, but giving no strength to perform it" (p. 383).

Then, Turretin addresses himself to the truth of the "Vocation of Reprobates." In keeping with his method of doing theology, he begins with a question in which he both sets forth the issue and indicates the direction in which he will go: "Are the Reprobate, who are made partakers of external vocation, called with the design and intention on God's part, that they should become partakers of salvation? And, this being denied, does it follow that God does not deal seriously with them, but hypocritically and falsely; or that he can be accused of any injustice? We deny" (p. 384).

Immediately, he draws the lines of battle: "This question lies between us and the Lutherans, the Arminians, and the Patrons of Universal Grace; who, to support the universality of vocation, at least as to the preaching of the Gospel in the visible Church, hold that as many as are called by the Word are called by God with the intention of their salvation; because otherwise God would trifle with men and deal not seriously but hypocritically, offering them grace, which, nevertheless, he is unwilling to bestow."

He then clarifies the position of Reformed orthodoxy: "Now although we do not deny that the reprobate, who live in external communion with the Church, are called by God through the Gospel; still we do deny that they are called with the intention that they should be made actual partakers of salvation, which God knew would never be the case, because in his decree he had ordained otherwise concerning them. Nor ought we on this account to think that God can be charged with hypocrisy or dissimulation, but that he always acts most seriously and sincerely" (pp. 384-385).

Thus does the Reformed faith cry down a plague on the houses of both hyper-Calvinism and the well-meant offer. Against hyper-Calvinism it maintains that God calls the reprobate through the preaching of the gospel and that He does so "most seriously and sincerely." Against the offer the Reformed faith denies that this call is made to the reprobate in mercy and with any design or intention of their salvation, and it denies this *in view of predestination:* "because in his decree he had ordained otherwise concerning them." Repudiation of the offer as the innovation of "Patrons of Universal Grace" is not hyper-Calvinism; it is historic Reformed orthodoxy.

Although the reprobate "are made partakers of external vocation," Turretin denies that they are called "with the design and intention on God's part, that they should become partakers of salvation." There are two reasons why they are called externally by God in the preaching of the gospel, neither of which is a sincere desire of God that they be saved. The first is that the reprobate "are mingled with the elect," so that "the Call cannot be addressed to men indiscriminately without the reprobate as well as the elect sharing in it." The second is God's purpose that the call of the reprobate accomplish their "conviction and inexcusability" (p. 385).

Turretin gives six grounds for the denial by Reformed orthodoxy that God calls the reprobate with the purpose that they partake of salvation: 1. "God cannot in calling intend the salvation of those whom He reprobated from eternity..."; 2. "God does not intend faith in the reprobate, therefore neither salvation which cannot be attained without faith"; 3. "Christ in the calling of the reprobate Jews testifies that He had as His proposed end their inexcusability" (Turretin here quotes John 9:39 and John 15:22); 4. "they who are called with the intention of salvation, are called *according to purpose,*" but only the elect are called thus, according to Romans 8:28ff., not the reprobate; 5. Salvation according to the intention of God is promised only to the weary and heavy laden (Matt. 11:28), the thirsty (Is. 55:1), and the believing and penitent (Acts 2:38), that is, the elect, not the reprobate; 6. God's promise is indeed that all who believe shall be saved, but God knows that the reprobate will never have faith, "nay, He, Who alone can give, has decreed to withhold (faith) from them." Therefore, it is "absurd to say that He calls the reprobate with the intention that they should be saved" (pp. 386, 387).

Just as is done by the advocates of the well-meant offer today, those in Turretin's day who defended a sincere intention of God to save all objected that, if God does not intend the salvation of all who are called in the gospel, God acts hypocritically and falsely. God is not truthful in calling a man to believe on Christ if He does not sincerely desire that man's salvation. The charge is made that those who deny a sincere desire of God to save every man who hears the gospel contradict the teaching of the Canons, that "as many as are called by the gospel are seriously called" (III, IV/8).

Turretin rejects this charge: "Although God does not intend the salvation of the reprobate by calling them, still He acts most seriously and sincerely, nor can any hypocrisy and deception be charged against Him." "The call to the reprobate is serious, because He seriously and most truly shows them the alone and most certain way of salvation, seriously exhorts them to

follow it, and most sincerely promises salvation to all
those who do follow it" (p. 387). The call is not hypocriti-
cal, or "feigned," to use the language of the Canons,
even though God has decreed that those called shall not
believe and shall not be saved, because the call to them
is a command, and "in such a command He wills to
unfold His right and man's duty" (p. 390). "For a serious
call does not require that there should be an intention
and purpose of drawing him, but only that there should
be a constant will of commanding duty, and bestowing
the blessing upon him who performs it, which God most
seriously wills" (p. 388).

Turretin turns the tables on the objectors. Not
Reformed orthodoxy, but those who maintain an intention of God to save all, while at the same time professing
the decree of reprobation, are guilty of ascribing hypocrisy and deception to God. For God to indicate to a man
in the gospel that He sincerely desires to save him when,
in fact, God has eternally decreed that man's damnation
is insincere, deceptive behavior.[6] "The opinion which
we oppose is far more strongly pressed with the same
difficulty. For on this hypothesis, God is made most
seriously to desire and intend the salvation of men
(provided they have faith) which yet he knows they
have not (and cannot have of themselves), and which he
himself decreed from eternity by an irrevocable decree
not to give (who alone can). It is easy to decide whether
this can be consistent with the sincerity of God. By this

---

6.   Similarly, God's sincerity is open to the most searching criticism if He proclaims to a man that He loves him, has given Christ
to die for his sins, and well-meaningly offers him salvation,
sincerely desiring to save him, but refuses sovereignly to regener-
ate that man and give him faith, presumably according to His own
will.

very thing, God is represented as testifying that he wills and does not will (at the same time) their salvation, because He does not will that without which it cannot be obtained (as if any one would say that he wills man to live, but yet nilled that he should breathe)."[7]

In conclusion, Turretin assures Reformed pastors that there is no substance to the dire predictions of the opponents that, without the doctrine of a sincere desire of God to save all men, lively, free, urgent preaching must decline. It is as if this representative of the Reformed faith in the seventeenth century could hear the "offer-men" of the twentieth century pronouncing their woes over those who insist that God's grace in the preaching is particular: "They cannot do mission work"; "they are unable to call everyone to repentance"; "they can preach only to the elect."

Without hesitation, Turretin asserts that the ministry of the gospel exists only for the sake of the elect: "For their (the elect's — DJE) sake alone the ministry of the gospel was instituted, to collect the church, and increase the mystical body of Christ, Eph. 4:12, and, they being taken out of the world, preaching would no longer be necessary..." (p. 385). This conviction, however, in no way hampers unfettered preaching: "Although the intention of Pastors' calling ought to be conformed to the intention of God, by Whom they are sent to call men; in this that they are bound from the order of God to invite all their hearers promiscuously to repentance and faith, as the alone way of salvation, and on condition of these to salvation; and they ought to intend nothing else than

---

7.   Turretin, *Institutes of Elenctic Theology*, ed. James T. Dennison, Jr., p. 415. There is evidently a mistake in the text of the Dennison edition: "as if anyone would say that he wills man to live, but yet willed that he should breathe." I have therefore, retained Turretin's original "nilled."

the gathering of the Church, or the salvation of the elect, in bringing about which they are co-workers with God: Still in this they also differ, that the omniscient God distinctly knows among gospel hearers, who are the elect, and who the reprobate. The former alone He wills to save individually, the latter not. Ministers, however, being destitute of such knowledge, do not know to whose salvation their ministry will contribute, not being able to distinguish between the elect and the reprobate, charitably hoping well for all, nor daring to decide concerning the reprobation of any one. Thus, they address all the called promiscuously and indiscriminately even by God's appointment, still intending the salvation of no others than the elect, like God. So that they do nothing in this ministry, which does not answer both to the command and intention of God..." (p. 389).

This would be enough to show that seventeenth century Reformed thought condemned the universal grace of the free offer theory. But there is more. Condemnation of the doctrine of universal grace in the call of the gospel and confession of particular grace did not remain confined to the writings of the theologians but were expressed in the confession of faith, the *Formula Consensus Helvetica* (Helvetic, or Swiss, Consensus Formula).

As is evident in the quotations, Turretin was not tilting at windmills when he opposed the doctrine of universal grace in the call of the gospel. Men within the Reformed camp were proclaiming this doctrine ("patrons of universal grace," Turretin called them). Just a few years after the Synod of Dordt and just a few years after the National Synod of the Reformed Church in France adopted the Canons of Dordt and bound all ministers and elders to defend them, theologians at the Reformed seminary in Saumur, France, began to attack the doctrine of sovereign grace, so recently explained and defended by the Dutch synod. The chief offender was Moyse Amyraut (or Moses Amyraldus). Amyraut taught that God has ordained all men unto salvation; that Christ died for all men; and that God offers Christ to all men, on the condition of faith, with a sincere intention to save them all. Grace, according to Amyraut, is universal.

The cloak under which Amyraut thought to smuggle this Arminian contraband into the Reformed churches was his profession of double predestination. However, he construed predestination as *following upon* the decree of universal salvation through universal atonement (all of which is dependent on man's acceptance or rejection of the offered grace) so that Amyraut's predestination was nothing other than the old Roman and Arminian doctrine of *conditional* predestination in new dress.

From the mountains of Geneva, Francis Turretin descried the enemy. With Lucas Gernler of Basle, he requested John Henry Heidegger of Zurich to compose a creed for the Swiss churches that would condemn the Saumur theology and pointedly affirm the decision of Dordt. Turretin helped Heidegger to write the creed. The result was the Helvetic Consensus Formula of 1675, "the last doctrinal Confession of the Reformed Church of Switzerland.[8] This confession was "agreed upon by the ecclesiastical and civil authorities of Zurich, Basle,

---

8. For a description of this creed and the theological controversy that gave rise to it, see Philip Schaff, *Creeds of Christendom* 1:477ff. Typically, Schaff calls it "a defense of the scholastic (sic!) Calvinism of the Synod of Dort." But it is, even in Schaff's reckoning, a defense of Dordt. It is "not so much intended to be a new confession of faith, as an explanatory appendix to the former Confessions...." Unfortunately, Schaff does not give the creed itself, only a very brief summary. The entire *Formula Consensus Helvetica* appears in

and Geneva, and adopted in other Reformed cantons as a binding rule of public teaching for ministers and professors."[9]

One cannot help noticing the striking fact that in those days (a flourishing period of Reformed theology), when the doctrine of predestination was questioned and assailed, the Reformed churches had recourse to the composition of a creed that reaffirmed and even buttressed (if this is possible) the Canons. Today, in the face of similar attacks, Reformed churches surrender the historic creeds, especially the Canons, so as to bring their confession into line with the unbelief of the heretics. Ours is not one of the most flourishing periods of Reformed theology.

A fascinating document, the Helvetic Consensus Formula confesses the verbal inspiration of the Scriptures, particularly the Old Testament, "not only in its consonants, but in its vowels — either the vowel points themselves, or at least the power of the points"; the imputation of Adam's sin; the federal Headship of Christ for the elect in the new covenant; limited atonement; and the covenant of works. It concludes with a decree "that we not only hand down sincerely in accordance with the Divine Word, the especial necessity of the sanctification of the Lord's Day, but also impressively inculcate it and importunately urge its observation." But our sole concern is its teaching regarding God's grace in the call of the gospel:

> Canon VI: Wherefore we can not give suffrage
> to the opinion of those who teach: (1) that

A.A. Hodge, *Outlines of Theology* (New York: Robert Carter and Brothers, 1879), "Appendix," pp. 656-663. The quotation that follows is taken from this source.
9.   Schaff, *Creeds of Christendom* 1:485, 486.

God, moved by philanthropy, or a sort of special love for the fallen human race, to previous election, did, in a kind of conditioned willing — willingness — first moving of pity, as they call it—inefficacious desire—purpose the salvation of all and each, at least conditionally, i.e., if they would believe; (2) that He appointed Christ Mediator for all and each of the fallen; and (3) that, at length, certain ones whom He regarded, not simply as sinners in the first Adam, but as redeemed in the second Adam, He elected, i.e., He determined to graciously bestow on these, in time, the saving gift of faith; and in this sole act Election properly so called is complete. For these and all other kindred teachings are in no wise insignificant deviations from the form of sound words respecting Divine election; because the Scriptures do not extend unto all and each God's purpose of showing mercy to man, but restrict it to the elect alone, the reprobate being excluded, even by name, as Esau, whom God hated with an eternal hatred (Rom. 9:10-13). The same Holy Scriptures testify that the counsel and the will of God change not, but stand immovable, and God in the heavens *doeth* whatsoever he will (Ps. 115:3; Is. 46:10); for God is infinitely removed from all that human imperfection which characterizes inefficacious affections and desires, rashness, repentance, and change of purpose.

Canon XVII: The call unto salvation was suited to its *due time* (I Tim. 2:6); since by God's will it was at one time more restricted, at another, more extended and general, but never absolutely universal. For, indeed, in the Old Testament God showed His word unto Jacob, His statutes and His judgments unto Israel; He dealt not so with any nation (Ps. 147:19, 20). In the New Testament, peace being made in the blood of Christ and the inner wall of partition broken down, God so extended the limits of Gospel preaching and the external call, that there is no longer any difference between the Jew and the Greek; for the same Lord over all is rich unto all that call upon Him (Rom. 9:12). But not even thus is the call universal; for Christ testifies that many are called (Matt. 20:16), not all; and when Paul and Timothy essayed to go into Bithynia to preach the Gospel, the Spirit suffered them not (Acts 16:7); and there have been and there are today, as experience testifies, innumerable myriads of men to whom Christ is not known even by rumor.

Canon XIX: Likewise the external call itself, which is made by the preaching of the Gospel, is on the part of God also, who calls, earnest and sincere. For in His Word He unfolds earnestly and most truly, not, indeed, His secret intention respecting the salvation or destruction of each individual, but what belongs to our duty, and what remains for us if we do or neglect this duty. Clearly it is the will of God who calls, that they who are called come to Him and not neglect so great salvation, and so He promises eternal life also in good earnest, to those who come to Him by faith; for, as the Apostle declares, "it is a faithful saying: For if we be dead with Him, we shall also live with Him; if we suffer, we shall also reign with Him; if we deny Him, He also will deny us; if we believe not, yet He abideth faithful; He cannot deny Himself." Nor in regard to those who do not obey the call is this will inefficacious; for God always attains that which He intends in His will, even the demonstration of duty, and following this, either the salvation of the elect who do their duty or the inexcusableness of the rest who neglect the duty set before them. Surely the spiritual man in no way secures the internal purpose of God to produce faith along with the externally proffered, or written Word of God. Moreover, because God approved every verity which flows from His counsel, therefore it is rightly said to be His will, that all who see the Son and believe on Him may have everlasting life (John 6:40). Although these "all" are the elect alone, and God formed no plan of universal salvation without any selection of persons, and Christ therefore died not for every one but for the elect only who were given to Him; yet He intends this in any case to be universally true, which follows from His special and definite purpose. But that, by God's will, the elect alone believe in the external call thus universally proffered, while the reprobate are hardened, proceeds solely from the discriminating grace of God: election by the same grace to them that believe; but their own native wickedness to the reprobate who remain in sin, and after their hardness and impenitent heart treasure up unto themselves wrath against the day of wrath, and revelation of the righteous judgment of God (Rom. 2:5).

Canon XX: Accordingly we have no doubt that they err who hold that the call unto salvation is disclosed not by the preaching of the Gospel solely, but even by the works of nature and Providence without any further proclamation; adding, that the call unto salvation is so indefinite and universal that there is no mortal who is not, at least objectively, as they say, sufficiently called either mediately, namely, in that God will further bestow the light of grace on him who rightly uses the light of nature, or immediately, unto Christ and salvation; and finally denying that the external call can be said to be serious and true, or the candor and sincerity of God be defended, without asserting the absolute universality of grace. For such doctrines are contrary to the Holy Scriptures....

Canon XXI: They who are called unto salvation through the preaching of the Gospel can neither believe nor obey the call, unless they are raised up out of spiritual death by that very power whereby God commanded the light to shine out of darkness, and God shines into their hearts with the soul-swaying grace of His Spirit....

This language is clear and sharp on the doctrine of the call of the gospel and the grace of God in the call, especially Canon XIX and the last part of Canon XX needing no explanation.

This is Turretin.

This is the Swiss churches of the seventeenth century.

And this is another reason why the noisy claim that the well-meant offer represents the position of the Reformed churches and theologians of the past does not so easily put us to ignominious flight. We too have read, and our finding is particular, sovereign grace in the preaching of the gospel.

Chapter 8
Kuyper's Doctrine of Particular Grace

It is widely assumed that the well-meant gospel offer, or free offer, has strong backing in the Dutch Reformed theologian Abraham Kuyper. Is not the crucial question in the controversy over the offer whether grace is common or particular? And did not Kuyper write a massive, three-volume work, *De Gemeene Gratie (Common Grace)*, in which he propounded the view that God has a favorable attitude towards all men and that a power of God works in all men restraining sin in the unbelieving world and enabling them to do much that is good and beautiful?[1] Certainly, then, those today who so vigorously propagate the offer stand in the line of the great Kuyper, whereas those who oppose the offer thereby place themselves outside the stream of historic Reformed theology as it developed in the Netherlands in the late 1800s.

This assumption is false.

It is indeed true that Kuyper taught a certain grace of God to all men, especially in his *De Gemeene Gratie*. It is also undoubtedly true that this teaching has been influential in the history of the Reformed faith from 1900 to the present day in the development of the theory of the well-meant offer of the gospel. But it is not true that Kuyper held the doctrine of the well-meant offer, not even in *De Gemeene Gratie;* on the contrary, he was an avowed foe of the theology of the offer.

---

1. Abraham Kuyper, *De Gemeene Gratie,* 3 vols. (Amsterdam: Höveker & Wormser, 1902-1904).

It is the express teaching of the doctrine of the offer that God is gracious to the reprobate with a grace that *sincerely desires their salvation* and that comes to them *in the gospel.* It is the implied teaching of the offer, where indeed this is not stated explicitly as is happening more and more in Reformed circles today, that Christ died for all men and that salvation depends upon man's acceptance of the offer by his free will.

Kuyper's common grace had nothing to do with this universal grace. The common grace of Kuyper was merely a favor of God that gives the world "the temporal blessings" of rain, sunshine, health, and riches and that restrains corruption in the world so that the world can produce good culture. It was not a grace that aimed at the salvation of the reprobate, a grace that was expressed in a well-meaning offer of Christ, or a grace that was grounded in a universal atonement. "Here now lies the root of the doctrine of 'common grace,' " wrote Kuyper: "There (is) in this sinful world, also outside the church, so much that is respectable, so much that arouses to jealousy.... To the good and beautiful outside the church, among unbelievers, in the world, we may not shut our eyes." The explanation of all this goodness in the world? "Outside the church, among the heathen, in the midst of the world, grace is working, grace which is not eternal, nor to the end of salvation, but which is temporal and to the end of checking the destruction that inheres in sin."[2]

Kuyper sharply distinguished this common grace from the saving grace of God. So concerned was he that "common grace" not be confused with "saving grace" (which is particular, according to Kuyper—for the elect

---

2. Abraham Kuyper, *De Gemeene Gratie,* 2d ed. (Kampen: J.H. Kok, n.d.), 1:11. The translation of the Dutch is mine.

only) that he deliberately gave "common grace" a name distinct from that of "particular grace." Common grace, he called *"gratie,"* whereas particular, saving grace was called *"genade."* Kuyper feared (prophetically, as history shows!) that misuse would be made of the doctrine of common grace, "as if *saving* grace were meant by it," with the result that "the firm foundation that grace *(genade)* is particular would again be dislodged." It is, however, "absolutely *not* the case" that common grace is saving grace. This may not "once be said of common grace." We must "guard against this vigorously and sharply *(kras en scherp)."* Common grace "does not contain a single saving germ and is, therefore, of a completely different nature than particular grace or covenant grace."[3]

Kuyper's attempt to prevent common grace from developing into universal, saving grace by giving the two graces different names was futile. The precarious co-existence of particular, saving grace and common, non-saving grace was shortlived. Soon common grace began nibbling on particular grace until by the present time it has almost completely devoured particular grace. The result is a "common grace" that sincerely desires the salvation of all and that expresses itself in offering Christ to all.

An outstanding and very clear instance of the fatal development of common grace into universal, saving grace is the first point of the doctrine of common grace adopted by the Christian Reformed Church in 1924. Beginning with Kuyper's distinction between two graces, "the saving grace of God shown only to those that are elect" and a "favorable attitude of God towards humanity in general and not only towards the elect," the first

---

3.   Ibid., pp. 8, 9.

point concludes by introducing common grace into the realm of salvation (the very error that Kuyper warned against), declaring that God's grace towards all humanity is revealed in the "general offer of the Gospel." No longer is common grace a favor that fills barns, fattens bellies, and produces Beethoven's *Fifth Symphony*, but it has become a favor that desires the salvation of all men and that operates towards all in the blessed gospel, offering all men eternal life.

Nor is this by any means an isolated instance. One finds on every hand that men ground their teaching of a grace of God for all in the preaching, that is, the well-meant offer, in God's common grace, thus transforming common (non-saving) grace into the universal (saving) grace of historic Romanism and Arminianism. In doing this, they are deaf to Kuyper's pleas not to make this mistake.

The Orthodox Presbyterian theologians Murray and Stonehouse were guilty of this. They were concerned to defend the free offer, the "real point" of which, according to their own analysis, is the teaching that "God desires the *salvation* of all men" (my emphasis — DJE). This grace, of course, "is expressed in the universal call to repentance," that is, the preaching of the gospel. But where did they begin when they looked for biblical support for this doctrine? Matthew 5:44-48! a passage which they themselves admitted "does not indeed deal with the overtures of grace in the gospel.... The particular aspect of God's grace reflected upon here is the common gifts of providence, the making of the sun to rise upon evil and good...." Nevertheless, this "common grace" in things temporal was made the foundation and source of the doctrine of a grace of God that desires salvation and that operates in the preaching. In the common grace of God "is disclosed to us a principle that applies to all manifestations of divine grace, namely, that the grace bestowed expresses the lovingkindness in the heart of God...."[4]

Erroll Hulse, the Calvinistic Baptist, propounds the same confusion without any of the carefulness of Murray and Stonehouse, who at least recognized that a grace that gives rain and a grace that offers salvation are two distinct things.[5] That Hulse intends to press common grace into the service of a universal grace in the gospel is indicated already in the title of his booklet: *The Free Offer: An exposition of common grace and the free invitation of the Gospel.* The content all too plainly confirms our suspicion. Hulse tells us that "the subject of common grace is inescapably connected with the free offer. It is not possible to deal adequately with the question of the offer without getting to grips with the subject of common grace" (pp. 4, 5). He is determined to arrive at the conclusion that God desires or wishes salvation for all and expresses this desire in the offer of salvation to all, that is, that God is gracious to all in the preaching. The premise on which this conclusion is based, according to Hulse, is common grace, God's favor to men in temporal things. Indeed, Hulse, nothing if not bold, goes so far as to identify common and special grace; there is no longer any qualitative difference between them. "Common grace finds its fullest expression in the provision of a Gospel to be addressed to all without exception" (p. 7). "Common grace, then, *finds its highest expression* in that desire and will of God not only for fallen man's temporal well-being, *but for his soul's salvation and eternal happiness*" (p. 8) (my emphasis —DJE). Apparently, it has never crossed Hulse's mind

4. Murray and Stonehouse, *The Free Offer of the Gospel,* pp. 3, 5-8, 26.
5. Hulse, *The Free Offer.*

that there might be a favor of God to men in earthly things without a grace that desires their salvation, as, in the view now of those who hold such a common grace, would have to be the case throughout the whole Old Testament time, when "the free invitation of the Gospel" to the heathen nations was not very conspicuous.

The confounding of "common grace" and "saving grace," particularly now by the appeal to common grace to prove the universal grace of the offer, has a profound, theological cause. Men simply cannot escape the overpowering testimony of the Scriptures that the grace of God is one, not two, and that this grace is the glorious favor of God towards damnworthy sinners that wills their deliverance from sin and death, provides redemption for them in the cross of the Beloved, and manifests itself in the gospel. If, then, there is a grace of God for all, men *must* conclude that the grace of God *in Christ Jesus* is for all. From this viewpoint, the Christian Reformed Church, the Orthodox Presbyterians, Erroll Hulse, and all their numerous allies are disciples of Abraham Kuyper in spite of themselves.

The only safeguard against universal, saving grace is the complete repudiation of Kuyperian common grace. Probably it is wishful thinking, but the startling appearance of outright universalism in Reformed churches today, universal atonement, universal redemptive love, universal election, and even universal salvation ought to make those who profess to love Reformed particularism reexamine the doctrine of common grace, uncritically accepted for so long as an aspect, even a basic aspect, of Reformed doctrine.[6]

6.   One could wish that Kuyper's *De Gemeene Gratie* were available in English, not because it has anything positive to contribute to Reformed theology but in order that many who swear by the doctrine of common grace, as by one of the fundamental articles of

But if Abraham Kuyper fathered the universal grace teaching of the well-meant offer, he did so as Lot fathered Moab and Ammon, unwittingly and unwillingly. Kuyper was an enemy of the teaching that is basic to the offer, namely, that God is gracious in the preaching to all men, the reprobate as well as the elect. Kuyper was a champion of the truth of particular, sovereign grace. He made this plain in his book *Dat de Genade Particulier is (That Grace is Particular.)*[7]

Abraham Kuyper wrote the book *Dat de Genade Particulier is,* because many were raising the motto, *"Christus pro omnibus* (Christ for all)," to a "shibboleth of evangelical truth." By this "Christ for all" was meant "that Christ, according to the intention and tendency of His self-offering, died for all men, head for head and soul for soul." Although the doctrine of universal atonement was on the foreground, Kuyper correctly saw that the real issue was the teaching that grace is common to all men. He refers to those who proclaim the doctrine of "Christ for all" as "zealots for common grace *(algemeene genade),"* and he opposes them by defending the fundamental proposition that grace is particular.[8]

Although those who confess particular grace are in the minority at present, Kuyper is encouraged to defend particular grace by the fact that "in earlier, and spiritu-

---

the Reformed faith, might see for themselves that the idol of common grace has feet of clay.

7.   Abraham Kuyper, *Dat de Genade Particulier is* (Amsterdam: J.H. Kruyt, 1884). Originally, the work was a series of articles that Kuyper wrote in the magazine *De Heraut* in 1878. Kuyper began the series on common grace in 1895, some seventeen years later. The quotations from *Dat de Genade Particulier is* that follow are my translation of the Dutch.

8.   Ibid., p. 3.

ally better, ages, I would have found plenty of allies."[9] He points to a "cloud of witnesses which did not know a grace which is not particular."[10] This cloud of witnesses includes Augustine, Calvin, Peter Martyr, Rivet, Voetius, Witsius, Beza, Zanchius, Gomarus, Turretin, and many others. Kuyper can safely say, without any exaggeration, that "in the time of our national glory, when there were still genuine theologians, and genuine theologians in quantity, shining in the church of these lands, the conviction 'that grace is particular' obtained as the only Biblical and Reformed position."[11] The teaching of "universal or common grace," on the other hand, which is the "doctrine of Rome, the Socinians, the Mennonites, the Arminians, and the Quakers, crept into the Reformed Churches from without, especially through Amyraut and the Saumur school."[12]

Kuyper wants to make sure that we understand what the issue is. The issue is not that those who confess particular grace affirm, whereas those who confess universal or common grace deny, that in the end only some are saved by the grace of God in Christ. For both parties acknowledge that only some are actually saved. But the issue concerns the will of God and the intention of Christ. Those who teach universal grace maintain that it is God's will and Christ's intention to save all men through Christ's death. "In contrast, the particularists ... teach: It must be preached by the church to every creature, that atonement has been obtained by the death of Christ for everyone who believed, believes, or will believe, that is, since all believers are the elect, only for

---

9.   Ibid., pp. 4, 5.
10. Ibid., p. 6.
11. Ibid., p. 14.
12. Ibid., pp. 13, 14.

the elect; and this is true, not merely according to the result, but according to Christ's intention and God's counsel. The Church must also preach that the atonement is applied, not to indefinite, as yet unconverted, persons, but to persons whom the Lord loves with an *eternal* love, already before they were born, and whom He 'calls by name.' "[13]

The advocates of universal grace in every age have three favorite texts: I John 2:2; I Timothy 2:4; and II Peter 3:9. Kuyper painstakingly explains these texts, rejecting the interpretation that makes them teach a grace of God towards every human being. "The three main texts with which men commonly like to scare the confessor of particular grace ... prove *nothing* (emphasis, as always, Kuyper's — DJE) for universal grace."[14]

Kuyper's explanation of II Peter 3:9 is typical. The text reads: "The Lord is not slack concerning his promise, as some men count slackness; but is longsuffering to usward, not willing that any should perish, but that all should come to repentance." In Kuyper's day as in ours, the popular interpretation of the text by the friends of universal grace (and foes of particular grace) is that God does not desire any member of the whole human race to perish but sincerely desires the salvation of all men without exception. Kuyper repudiates this interpretation not only as heterodoxy but also as folly. "For then I come to this absurd reasoning: 'Jesus *cannot* yet come, because God's will must be fulfilled, and, according to God's will, all men must first come to repentance. But ... if Jesus cannot come, until all men come to repentance, *then Jesus will never come*. For, first, there are already hundreds and thousands of dead people, who died

13. Ibid., p. 27.
14. Ibid., p. 69.

unconverted.... Second, there are millions upon millions who will die today, tomorrow, or next year, without ever having heard of Jesus.... And finally, if God, without a definite goal, simply allows new men to be born continuously, and the coming of Jesus then must be delayed, until also these are converted, that coming of Jesus can be delayed endlessly....' " The explanation of II Peter 3:9 that holds that God desires to save all men involves "the most absurd reasoning imaginable and is utterly senseless."[15]

"In II Peter 3:9, nothing else can be meant than this: Jesus cannot come before the number of the elect is full, and, inasmuch now as many elect have not yet been converted, He delays His coming, in His longsuffering, not willing that some would go lost through a premature return, but willing that they all first be converted."[16] In the light cast by the history of the Reformed struggle to defend sovereign, particular grace, it is clear that the explanation one gives of II Peter 3:9 can well serve as the touchstone of a genuinely Reformed confession of the grace of God.

Having disposed of the superficial explanation of a few texts commonly opposed to the truth of particular grace, Kuyper proceeds to expose the error of the teaching that God is gracious to all men. His first argument is that the doctrine of total depravity refutes the notion of universal grace. Kuyper's reasoning here is well

---

15. One can hear the men whose position Kuyper here demolishes assuring themselves and their followers that Kuyper is "too logical." In that case, it will at least be evident from the passage that it is historically Reformed to be logical in explaining God's truth. Those in the Reformed camp today who recommend absurdity should advise us of their origins.
16. Kuyper, *Dat de Genade Particulier is*, p. 64.

worth noting. He argues that universal grace necessarily implies the ability of the sinner to accept that intended and offered grace, that is, implies the heresy of free will. All that is necessary, therefore, to disprove the contention of universal grace and to establish the truth of particular grace is the demonstration from the Scriptures that the natural man is totally depraved, incapable of accepting any offer of salvation.

"If it be true, what the proponents of universal grace teach, namely, that grace is offered to all men, head for head, on the ground that, in fact and really, the ransom is already paid for them, then it must herewith be supposed that the sinner, as he is in sin, yet possesses a power, an ability, a possibility in his soul, *to accept* the salvation offered to him." "If one teaches over against this, 'No, the sinner is not able to do that. He has sunk away too deeply for that, and, for him to be able to do that, something must first happen *in him,* by which he receives the power to lay hold on that offered (presented — DJE) salvation,' then, obviously, 'universal grace' is found to be completely untenable on account of this one confession (of total depravity — DJE), because, in fact, *not all* men receive 'this possibility to be able to believe' by a particular grace."[17]

"Of an *intention* in God at the forming of the plan of salvation and the carrying out of that plan in the death of Christ *to save all sinners* head for head, there can, therefore, be no mention, unless God knew that all these sinners yet retained the might, the power, and the ability ... to believe in Jesus Christ and in the redemption through His blood."[18]

---

17. Ibid., pp. 70, 71.
18. Ibid., p. 92.

The preceding quotation with its reference to God's intention indicates that Kuyper's opposition to universal grace not only concerns the teaching that Christ died for all men but also concerns the teaching that there is an intention of God to save all. This is a basic element of the present-day doctrine of the well-meant offer of the gospel. Kuyper concentrates on this aspect of the error of universal grace when he goes on to show that the theory of universal grace is in conflict with what the Scriptures teach concerning "the Being and perfections of God."

Those in the Reformed camp who teach that God is gracious to all must acknowledge that God knows, indeed has decreed, that only some will be saved. How then can they say that God wills or desires to save all? Their answer, says Kuyper, is the contention that there is a distinction between two wills of God: "One asserts then that 'will' and 'decree' are to be distinguished." What they mean is that there are two opposite, conflicting wills in God: He wills to save all, and He wills not to save all. "That," writes Kuyper, "is gibberish *(wartaal)....* To place in one and the same decree 'yes' and 'no' at the same time is to ascribe to God something absurd, a thing that must be resisted with all our might."

It is, of course, true that there is a proper distinction to be made between God's "will" and God's "decree." But this is the distinction between what God commands men to do and what God Himself decided to do. "God's will is: Thou shalt not kill; but in His counsel the murder of our William the First is included. God's will is: Thou shalt not commit adultery; and yet Bathsheba is foreordained to be the mother of Solomon.... Certainly, if there is mention of the will of God *which must be a directive for us men* in our actions, then, of course, this revealed will of God is nothing else than His holiness mirrored in His commandments and which, therefore, has nothing to do with His decree or with His counsel." But this is not at all what the defenders of universal grace have in mind with their distinction between two wills in God. They do not refer to "what God wills that the *man* should do," but they are speaking of "a counsel and plan that *God Himself* carries out." "There would be then, on the one hand, a will of God, that He Himself shall work at the salvation of all, and, on the other hand, a will of God, that He Himself carry out a plan according to which not all shall be saved." This, says Kuyper, is "gibberish," unworthy of Reformed theology and an attack on the Being and perfections of God.[19]

It is incontrovertibly clear that Reformed theology will not permit those who maintain both a sincere desire of God to save all and the decree of election, that is, the defenders of the offer, to find any refuge in their distinction between two wills in God. The "paradox" behind which they hide at the crucial moment is not a biblical, Reformed "paradox," but absurdity, absurdity which serves to introduce conflict into the Being and decree of God and the heresy of universal grace into the Reformed churches. The distinction between a will of God that desires and intends to save all and a will of God that does not desire and intend to save all is a spurious distinction and one that Reformed theology has not only not recognized but explicitly condemned. The God Who commands all who hear the gospel to repent and believe is a God Who wills, desires, and intends the salvation of the elect and the elect alone.

As the next step in his "apology for particular grace," Kuyper goes through the entire Bible showing "that the

---

19. Ibid., pp. 102-105.

Holy Scripture indeed teaches particular grace."[20] He
covers the Old Testament in three stages, the period
from Adam to Noah, the period from the patriarchs to
Moses, and the period of the prophets. His conclusion
is this: "Plainly, exceedingly plainly, it appears that if
we put the question to God Himself, how *He* has intended His grace, neither His operations of grace nor
His gracious promises (as far as the Old Testament is
concerned, at any rate) give us even the least right to
speak of a grace which, according to the counsel and
according to the provisions and *according to the revealed
will of God,* would be intended for the salvation of the
entirety of all human individuals" (my emphasis —
DJE). In the Old Testament Scriptures "without any
ambiguity, there is the very definite testimony of a grace
which is not universal, but particular."[21]

But what does the New Testament say "about the
common or particular character of grace"? "What is
revealed to us concerning this in and through Jesus?"
Kuyper limits himself at this point to the gospels. Matthew, Mark, and Luke teach that "Jesus preached that
salvation proceeds according to *election* and ... repeat-
edly, and expressly distinguished the elect from the
non-elect." The synoptics also teach "that the blood of
Jesus will be shed, not for *all,* but for *many*"; and "that
those who obtain salvation do not obtain it according to
an uncertain result, but according to the holy predestination of God." God's grace in Christ is not even
intended for every Israelite. Kuyper makes a distinction
between an elect kernel and a reprobate husk: "Jesus,
like the prophets, very sharply distinguishes the spiritual kernel in Israel from the unholy mass. Not to all

20. Ibid., p. 162.
21. Ibid., pp. 191, 192.

Israel was He sent, but only to the 'lost sheep of the house of Israel.' " The gospel of John teaches the same truth, so that the conclusion must be "that the doctrine of 'common grace' can in no way or manner be harmonized with that which was spoken by Jesus. On the other hand, particular grace was taught by Jesus in the plainest words."[22]

Inevitably, defense of the truth that God is gracious only to the elect raises the question whether the gospel is to be preached to all men without distinction and, if so, why? This question arises from two quarters. On the one hand, those who hold that God is gracious to all men raise the question as an argument against the truth of particular grace. By this question they mean to say, "If grace is particular, the church cannot preach the gospel to all men, as she is called to do." On the other hand, there are those, the hyper-Calvinists, who deduce from the doctrine of particular grace that the church should preach only to the regenerated elect. Kuyper confronts this crucial question in a chapter entitled "To Whom (Must the Gospel Be) Preached?": "Now we have come to the question, whether the gospel of Christ must be preached to every soul, or only to the elect?"[23]

Kuyper's answer is: "to *every soul* without distinction; God does *not* will any limitation of the preaching to the elect." This is not an unimportant matter to Kuyper; he roundly condemns every effort to restrict the gospel: "And so entirely foreign to us is the limiting of gospel-preaching, that we rather condemn as unlawful and unbiblical every attempt somehow to fence in the preaching of the gospel."[24]

---

22. Ibid., pp. 193-214.
23. Ibid., p. 292.
24. Ibid., pp. 292, 293.

As if he lived at the end of the twentieth century with its corruptions of preaching, all under the name of evangelism, Kuyper finds it necessary to add that he does not mean "that we recognize as gospel-preaching, everything that claims to be gospel-preaching; nor that we acknowledge as gospel-*preachers* everyone that sets himself up as a gospel-preacher: nor that we approve every *method* by which men think that they have to preach the gospel. On the contrary, we understand by gospel-preaching only 'the proclamation of the whole counsel of God,' by persons lawfully qualified thereto and in the manner prescribed by the Word of God" — a description of gospel-preaching that warms the cockles of a Reformed heart.[25] Nevertheless, "of such a gospel-preaching we say that it may not aim only at the elect, but that the preaching of reconciliation must direct itself towards everything that is sinner *(tot al wat zondaar is).*"[26]

But why? Why must the gospel be preached to *all*, when God's grace, in that very gospel, is not for all but for some, the elect, only? The answer that many give to this question undermines everything else that they might say about a decree of election, particular redemption, total depravity, and irresistible grace. Their answer is: "because God loves them all, reprobate as well as elect; because God sincerely desires the salvation of all, the non-elect as well as the elect; and because God's love moves Him to make a well-meant offer to all." In other words, their answer is: "because God, after all, is gracious to all." Thus, the dike of particular grace, no

---

25. Similarly heartwarming is Kuyper's description of the proper motive in preaching the gospel: "The Gospel must be preached, not out of ambition, in order to say, 'I have been able to save souls'; but *out of obedience to God"* (p. 298).
26. Ibid., p. 293.

matter how laboriously strengthened at other points, is breached, and the waters of universal (ineffectual) grace inundate the Reformed land.

This, however, is not Kuyper's answer!

That the gospel must be preached to all "stands fast on a threefold basis," no aspect of which is a grace of God to all or a desire of God to save all.

The first reason for preaching to all is this, that "God's Word nowhere contains a limitation under the New Covenant; rather it lays emphasis on the falling away of every limitation; and actually shows us the preaching of the gospel to all sinners...." "Both John the Baptist and the apostles preached the gospel in the synagogue, without the least limitation." Especially the preaching of Jesus is proof, for, although He was the one Preacher Who knew who were elect and who were reprobate, He preached to all.[27]

The second reason is that we "cannot distinguish the sheep from the goats." Preaching is intended by God to gather the elect, but we do not know who the elect are. Therefore, we must preach to all. An implication, says Kuyper, is that "the doctrine of election, rather than restricting the extent of the preaching, offers the strongest incentive to bring the preaching to all."[28]

There is a third reason. This has to do with the fact that God has a purpose in bringing the Word to the reprobate. "It is ... altogether misconceived, if one says: God lets His gospel be preached to all sinners with the exclusive purpose, that it come to His elect.... Rather, even if all the elect stood on one side and all the lost stood on the other side, the high, serious obligation would still rest on the Church of Jesus to cause *both* to hear the

27. Ibid., p. 295.
28. Ibid., pp. 295, 297.

gospel." For "to these (elect) we are indeed a savour of
life unto life, *but we are also a savour of death unto death unto
the others;* and the preacher of the gospel, *also when he
brings death,* is a good savour unto God. This is what
Paul expressly says in II Corinthians 2:15: 'We are unto
God a sweet savour of Christ, in them that are saved, *and
in them that perish.'* "[29]

God intends to convict the lost sinner of the extent of
his depravity. The sinner likes to contradict God's
judgment on him that he is totally depraved. But the
awful depths of his depravity are made undeniably
plain exactly when he laughs at and rejects the redemption presented to him in the gospel. "It is for this reason,
so that He may appear righteous that God now has the
ransom presented *(aanbieden,* 'offer, present' — DJE) to
every creature without distinction." "The preaching of
the cross of Jesus must indeed properly be brought to the
lost, as well as to the *elect,* so that the sinner may be
convicted of guilt and God may be justified in His
ways."[30]

Although the gospel must be preached to all, the
content of preaching may not be an announcement that
the grace of the gospel is for all. Kuyper will not permit
a preacher to say to everyone in his audience, "The
ransom has been obtained for you," that is, Christ died
for you (or, by implication, God loves you). "Whenever
you stand as a teacher before a *Christian congregation,*
then you may and must say that (namely, the ransom
has been obtained for you — DJE), as often as you
address the *congregation as a whole....* But, on the contrary, when you do not speak in a congregation ... and
thus simply address sinners, then you may and must

29. Ibid., pp. 298, 299.
30. Ibid., pp. 300, 301.

say, 'Salvation has appeared *for every one who believes....*' "

"The presentation *(aanbieding)* of this ransom in such a way that you say, 'It is destined for you personally,' can only be preached to the congregation of Christ or to one who shows himself to you as converted in his heart. Whereas the preaching of the ransom of Christ also to those who go lost must abide by the explicit rule which is described by the holy apostle Paul in this manner: 'to the one a savour of life unto life, to the other a savour of death unto death'; but the preacher is 'unto God a sweet savour of Christ both in them that are saved, and in them that perish.' "[31]

This was Abraham Kuyper's clear exposition and powerful defense of the Reformed faith at a crucial moment in the history of that faith in the Netherlands. He did this in the face of great opposition. For 140 years the theologians at home and abroad had exerted all their powers to obliterate the truth of particular grace with the result that almost all pastors had forgotten the doctrine and public opinion in the church held it for foolishness. Kuyper's colleagues cursed him from their pulpits: "Whoever preaches another gospel than that Christ died for all men, let him be accursed." Even his friends urged him not to write a defense of particular grace, at least not so early in the movement. It would alienate the "weaker brethren," hurt the cause of the newly created *De Heraut (The Herald,* the magazine in which Kuyper and his cohorts spread their views and in which the articles on particular grace originally appeared), and jeopardize the plans for the Free University.

Nevertheless, he wrote. The reason? Kuyper tells us the reason. He was concerned "for the favor and the

31. Ibid., pp. 302, 305, 306.

grace of the Lord our God, more than for the favor of men." "Exactly through the confession of particular grace, the worth of His glory and the infinite fulness of His divine favor reveals itself to our soul's eye...." "It would have been beneath God's dignity and a disparagement of His honor, and would be found altogether loveless and powerless in our God, to offer to poor creatures, who lay cast away in their need, nothing than a *chance* at an *uncertain* salvation; to allow His beloved Son to die at the risk that, perhaps, His holy blood would be shed for nothing; and to keep His dear children on earth in anguish and fear, right up to the last gasp, that, perhaps, all will still be lost — no, brothers, that you cannot, that you may not believe any longer, and if you do believe that, Oh, how you grieve and how you belittle the honor of the love and the mercy of the Lord our God!"[32]

We hear much of Kuyper today. The Kuyper of common grace and the Kuyper of a "Reformed world-and-life-view" is proclaimed and acclaimed in the Reformed sphere. But from all the disciples of Kuyper and from the "new-Kuyperians" very little is heard of the Kuyper of particular grace. Indeed, of this Kuyper, the *essential* Kuyper, we hear nothing.

Strange.

---

32. Ibid., pp. 448-452.

Chapter 9
The Threat of Hyper-Calvinism

The question must now be faced whether the Reformed doctrine of the call of the gospel is actually threatened by the error of hyper-Calvinism. Does the denial of the well-meant offer have to exert itself to ward off the danger of restricting the preaching of the gospel to born again believers, the danger of silencing the call to sinners to repent and believe, and the danger of losing zeal for missions?

Hyper-Calvinism is not the predominant evil of our time. The man who has an eye for the overthrow of the doctrine of God's sovereign, particular grace in the Reformed sphere today is inclined to regard the hue and cry raised against hyper-Calvinism as a display of ignorance at best or a subterfuge at worst. As the Reformed house goes up in flames, the watchers alert us to the peril of flooding, call for lifeboats, and give swimming lessons. The same folly occurs in society. As society goes under in lawlessness and immorality, the supposed guardians of society decry the evils of a strait-laced, "Puritan" morality. In view of the advance of Arminianism in the past fifty years, especially in the area of "evangelism" and the call of the gospel, one is tempted to propose fifty years of hyper-Calvinism as a radical measure to check the wildfire spread of the free-will cancer.

This temptation, of course, must be decisively rejected. Error cannot be fought with error but only with the truth. The Reformed faith has always been characterized by a refusal to become reactionary. It has never allowed heresy to drive it into the opposite error. It will not engage in theology or preach out of fear. Steadfastly, it insists on being biblical.

The outstanding example of this is the Synod of Dordt. The Reformed churches were confronted with the false doctrine of man's salvation of himself by his free will. Basic to this error was the teaching that the preaching of the gospel is God's gracious effort to save every man. The Reformed fathers viewed this error as a perversion of the gospel, the destruction of the Reformed churches, and the robbery of the glory of God in His greatest work, the work of salvation.

The vehemence of their opposition to the Arminian heresy might have led the fathers to react by slighting the importance of the preaching of the gospel and by denying the serious call of God to everyone to whom the gospel comes. But such was not at all the case. The presence and power of the Holy Spirit at that "most holy Synod," leading the church into all the truth, are evident, in no small way, in its firm emphasis on the unique importance of the preaching of the gospel as the means of grace and in its unwavering insistence on the serious call by God and His church to every person to whom God sends the gospel.

The approach of the Canons is that of the necessity of the preaching for the saving of lost sinners. They open by declaring that some men are delivered from the common misery by the preaching of the joyful tidings of the cross of Christ (I/1-4). They make the calling of the elect unto salvation through the preaching of the gospel part of the decree of election itself (I/7). For the assurance of election and salvation they shut the children of God up to the preaching (I/12, 16; V/10). Even though the Arminians pervert this truth, deceiving many, the Canons are not at all embarrassed by the declaration that the promise of the gospel is that "whosoever believeth" shall be saved, nor do they hesitate to charge the Reformed churches and preachers to publish this promise to all nations and persons, "promiscuously and without distinction," and to command all men to repent and believe (II/5). This call is God's serious call to all who hear the preaching, and those who reject it have themselves alone to blame (III,IV/8, 9). The sovereignty of God's grace in the actual quickening of the dead sinner, confessed by the Canons over against the Arminian teaching of a mere persuasion of the co-operating sinner, "in no wise," the Canons are quick to add, "excludes, or subverts the use of the gospel, which the most wise God has ordained to be the seed of regeneration, and food of the soul." God uses means, and, therefore, any separation of sovereign grace from "the sacred precepts of the gospel" is nothing less than the sin of tempting God (III, IV/17). The preaching of the gospel is the necessary means of grace for the elect to the very end: "And as it hath pleased God, by the preaching of the gospel, to begin this work of grace in us, so he preserves, continues, and perfects it by the hearing and reading of his Word, by meditation thereon, and by the exhortations, threatenings, and promises thereof, as well as by the use of the sacraments" (V/14).

Also of this aspect of the instruction of the Canons the Reformed believer and the Reformed church must be good and faithful students.

For the threat of hyper-Calvinism is real. It is the lie on the right that must be guarded against as scrupulously as the lie of self-salvation on the left. The reality of the threat is indicated, first, by the history of the church. Church history contains a Hussey and a Brine, who, in the name of Calvinism and the doctrines of grace, denied that the call of the gospel in its external aspect comes to any save the elect and who charged

those who called all men indiscriminately to repent of
their sins and believe on Jesus Christ with Arminianism.
These theologians have disciples today. Granted, these
English hyper-Calvinists were not ecclesiastically Reformed. Nevertheless, since they claimed to be Calvinists and since others regarded them as Calvinists, they
have had influence in the sphere of Reformed theology.
Besides, evidence is not altogether lacking that the
hyper-Calvinistic error has appeared in the Reformed
churches in the Netherlands. It is at least questionable
whether opposition to the Arminian offer has not sometimes taken the form of a denial of the serious call of the
gospel to any and all to whom the gospel comes, reprobate as well as elect.

Certainly, a reading of the histories of the Reformed
churches in the Netherlands after the Secession of 1834
reveals a struggle over the doctrine of the call of the
gospel. There has not always been perfect clarity concerning this doctrine, any more than there has always
been perfect clarity concerning the truth of the covenant;
there is development in the understanding and confession of the truth. Men struggled with the question "If
God has elected some and reprobated others, if Christ
died only for the elect and not for the non-elect, if God's
desire is the saving of the elect only, and if the Arminian
teaching of an offer of salvation to all is false, can the
preaching of the gospel be a serious call to repentance
and faith to everyone who hears it?" "How can a serious
call to all men be harmonized with election and particular grace?" "And is there not a danger that an insistence
on the serious call to everyone will open up the way once
more to the introduction of the hated Arminian heresy?"

It is not difficult to conceive that someone would
conclude that the defense of sovereign grace and the
warding off of Arminianism demand a minimizing, a

silencing, or even a denying of the promiscuous proclamation of the gospel and the serious call of the gospel to
all hearers. No doubt, this was exactly the motivation of
the English hyper-Calvinists. But error remains error,
no matter how "sincere" the motive, and the consequences of error are not a whit abated because the
motives are "honorable."

Nor are we ignorant of Satan's devices. The appearance of the error of hyper-Calvinism in the history of the
church cannot simply be ascribed to the frailty of theologians but must be traced back to the father of the lie.
Where the truth is and where, under the guidance of the
Holy Spirit, the truth is being developed, there the Devil
will also be found working. He is subtle. If he cannot
prevent the recovery of the gospel of grace, he will try
to turn grace into license. If he fails to destroy the
Reformed faith with the doctrine of universal grace,
dependent upon the will of man — the well-meant offer
— he will endeavor to pervert this faith by a denial of the
serious call of the gospel to all hearers and by a question-
ing of the church's duty and right to bring this command
to all nations and to all persons promiscuously and
without distinction. This tactic is especially effective in
the heat of controversy. As the church contends against
a false doctrine, get her to succumb in reaction to the
opposite error. As she guards the front door, slither in
through the back window.

It does not surprise us that the Reformed faith has
been threatened by the stultifying, deadening error of
hyper-Calvinism. Indeed, we would be surprised if this
were not the case. But we thank God that it has
repudiated this error as vigorously as it has repudiated
the error of free-will.

The reality of the threat of hyper-Calvinism is also
indicated by the Scriptures. The Scriptures warn that

the gospel of grace has two outstanding enemies: the teaching that man saves himself by his own working or willing and the teaching that salvation by grace alone implies carelessness of life or even licentiousness. As Toplady wrote somewhere, in his characteristically vivid manner: "Christ is still crucified between two thieves, Antinomism and Pharisaism." Those who know and love the truth must beware of the former error as well as the latter.

Strictly speaking, antinomism is the heresy that denies that the believer ought to obey the law of God. The word itself is composed of two Greek words "anti," which means "against," and "nomos," which means "law." It refers to a teaching that is opposed to the law of God. Specifically, the teaching is opposed to the law of God as the rule of the thankful life of the redeemed child of God. Since God's people are saved by grace alone, the antinomian argues, they need not obey the law; indeed, it is treason to the gospel to command God's people to keep the commandments. Although the antinomian would allow for the law's function of teaching men their misery, he opposes that use of the law which consists of its being a positive standard for holy living. When he appears in the Reformed tradition (as he does!) he is very strong on the first part of the Heidelberg Catechism and very weak on the third part.

Essential to this false doctrine is its opposition to the law *in the name of the gospel*. It does not simply reject the law as the ungodly world also rejects the law, but it rejects the law *because the people of God are saved by grace without the works of the law*. Thus, the gospel of grace itself is made the ground of laxity and immorality.

The Scriptures both warn that this error will always harass the gospel and pass judgment upon it as false doctrine. Already in the Old Testament the prophet

Jeremiah had to contend with Israelites who declared, "We are delivered to do all these abominations," that is, steal, murder, commit adultery, and practise idolatry (Jer. 7:9, 10). The Word of the Lord condemned this doctrine as "lying words, that cannot profit" (Jer. 7:8).

Antinomism is explicitly repudiated by Paul. In Romans 3:31 he asks, "Do we then make void the law through faith?" Having proclaimed a righteousness by faith only, altogether apart from man's works, he asks in Romans 6:1 whether this doctrine implies wickedness of life: "What shall we say then? Shall we continue in sin, that grace may abound?" Again, his answer is a ringing renunciation of the antinomian error: "God forbid. How shall we, that are dead to sin, live any longer therein?" (v. 2). He admonishes the Galatian saints not to use the liberty of grace for an occasion to the flesh, but to exercise liberty in the only appropriate way, namely, by the keeping of God's law (Gal. 5:13, 14).

In a broader sense, antinomism is the error that interprets God's sovereignty as the weakening or denial of man's responsibility and that applies the truth of sovereign grace in such a way as to minimize or deny the calling of the church and of the saved sinner. It is this that constitutes the error of hyper-Calvinism. Many would-be critics of hyper-Calvinism fail to see this. They think to find hyper-Calvinism's essential error in an overemphasis on the sovereignty of God, especially in the work of salvation. Accordingly, one alleges that it is supralapsarianism that constitutes hyper-Calvinism; another puts the finger on eternal justification; and still another identifies the culprit as the doctrine of an unconditional covenant. The effect of these critics' going to war against "an overemphasis on the sovereignty of God" is that they become foes, not of hyper-Calvinism but of Calvinism itself.

Anglican theologian Peter Toon is one who finds the characteristic error of hyper-Calvinism in an over-emphasis on the sovereignty of God. Toon refers to Herman Hoeksema as the outstanding modern hyper-Calvinist because Hoeksema "places excessive emphasis on the sovereign grace of God."[1] Had Toon charged Hoeksema with an *exclusive* emphasis on the sovereignty of God, so that he denied or minimized the responsibility of man, we would have to take Toon's charge seriously. Since the charge is that of "excessive" emphasis, we can ignore it. For it is impossible to emphasize the sovereignty of God excessively, especially as regards the sovereignty of grace. Stand before the incarnation, the cross, and the wonder of regeneration, and try to de-emphasize sovereign grace! The "charge" that a theologian excessively emphasizes sovereign grace is in fact the highest praise that one can give that theologian, praise that identifies him as a faithful servant of the gospel of the grace of God in Christ Jesus.

One cannot emphasize the sovereignty of God strongly enough! The all-out emphasis on the almighty sovereignty of Jehovah God is the truth and beauty of Calvinism. Nor can one stress sufficiently that the salvation of God's elect is from beginning to end a matter of sovereign, free grace! The emphatic proclamation of sovereign grace is the power and comfort of Calvinism. Touch this, and you are not guarding against hyper-Calvinism but rather are creating Pelagianism and Arminianism. Not in an emphasis on God's sovereignty but in a denial of man's responsibility must the characteristic flaw of hyper-Calvinism be located.

---

1. Peter Toon, "Hyper-Calvinism," in *Encyclopedia of the Reformed Faith*, ed. Donald K. McKim (Louisville, Kentucky: Westminster/John Knox Press, 1992), p. 190.

It must be quickly added that the mere fact that a man or a church is charged with hyper-Calvinism does not prove that the man or the church is, indeed, guilty of the heresy. Hyper-Calvinism, we have said, is a form of antinomism, and the Scriptures teach that every defender of the sovereignty of God's grace in salvation will be falsely accused of antinomism. Of Paul himself it was reported, though slanderously, that he taught the doctrine "Let us do evil, that good may come" (Rom. 3:8), the sheer falsity of which slander is shown in Romans 6, 8, and 12-16.

Such has ever been one of Rome's main attacks on the Reformed faith: the preaching of *sola gratia* makes men careless and profane. Again and again, the Reformed creeds refer to this charge in order to repudiate it. Question 64 of the Heidelberg Catechism is an instance. Regarding the truth of justification by faith alone, the Catechism asks: "But doth not this doctrine make men careless and profane?" The answer: "By no means: for it is impossible that those, who are implanted into Christ by a true faith, should not bring forth fruits of thankfulness."

In a way, the label "Antinomian — Hyper-Calvinist," tagged on the staunch Calvinist by Calvinism's open or secret enemies, is a badge of honor, much as the Calvinist repudiates the charge. So labelled (libelled, really!), he stands in good company, the company of all those who have ever consistently and uncompromisingly stood for the sovereignty of God and salvation by pure grace.

We cannot ignore, in this connection, the allegation that a denial of human responsibility appeared in the theology of Herman Hoeksema. A.C. DeJong supposed that he saw this in a well-known and much reported statement by Hoeksema: "I always say, beloved: Give

me God, if I must make a choice. If I must make a choice
to lose God or man, give me God. Let me lose man. It's
all right to me: no danger there. Give me God! That's
Reformed! And that's especially Protestant Reformed!"[2]

But this dramatic "here I stand" in no way represented a denial or even a weakening of the biblical truth
of man's responsibility. The statement occurred in an
address given in June, 1953, in the heat of the battle of the
Protestant Reformed Churches against the doctrine of a
conditional covenant and a conditional promise. The
doctrine with which Hoeksema was contending was not
an affirmation of man's responsibility, not even a *strong*
affirmation of man's responsibility, but a denial of
sovereign grace. However, the denial of God's sovereignty was being introduced in the guise of a defense of
man's responsibility. In that context and in the heat of
that battle, when not only the Protestant Reformed
Churches but also the truth of sovereign grace was at
stake, Hoeksema cried out, "Give me God, *if* I must
make a choice. *If* I must make a choice to lose God or
man, give me God." The man who does not recognize
in this trumpet blast the call to give glory to God in the
face of another assault on that glory by man, and thrill
to it, is to be pitied.

The sentence that immediately precedes, not quoted
by DeJong, refers to "the Pelagian, *that always emphasizes
man rather than God*" (my emphasis — DJE). In contrast
to the Pelagian, Hoeksema will emphasize God rather
than man. In no way is the statement a denial of human
responsibility. The entire address is exactly the presentation in clear, strong terms of the historic Reformed
teaching of the full responsibility of both fallen and

---

2. Quoted by A.C. DeJong, *Well-Meant Gospel-Offer*, p. 81.

saved men, and is well worth reading on this account.[3]

Fact is, Reformed theologians have made the very same point in almost the very same language down through the ages. Abraham Kuyper is an example. In the course of his defense of particular grace, he writes that "those who reject particular grace, on their part, give *man* his due, but only so that they may detract from that which is *God's* due.... In order to maintain the moral attributes of man inviolate, they abandon part of the attributes of the Being of the living God. Over against this, we would now allow ourselves this question: If you are not able to harmonize the activity of men and the activity of God in the work of salvation, and for this reason you suppose that you have to take away something either from man or from God, would it then not be more humble for man, more appropriate, and safer, rather to give himself up than in the slightest to detract anything from the inviolability of the Being and the attributes of God? And if this would appear advisable to you in general, does this not become a yet much stronger obligation, when there is mention no longer of man's inviolability, but of the activity of *a sinner*, that is, of a human being, which is *no longer* sound and undamaged? This leads to the conclusion that if something must be abandoned, either from our side or from God's side, the man who fears God is always inclined rather to give up everything of himself than to take away even one thing from the full and inviolate Majesty of his God."[4]

This sounds familiar: "The modernistic Pelagian always emphasizes man rather than God. I always say,

3. Herman Hoeksema, "Man's Freedom and Responsibility," *Standard Bearer* 29 (July 1, 1953), pp. 412-417.
4. Kuyper, *Dat de Genade Particulier is,* pp. 326, 327.

beloved: Give me God, if I must make a choice. If I must make a choice to lose God or man, give me God.... Give me God: there is no salvation in man!"

This is Reformed language. It is the language, as Kuyper says, of the man who fears God. To interpret this language now as a denial of man's responsibility is enough to make one who knows Abraham Kuyper and Herman Hoeksema smile.

Nevertheless, a denial of man's responsibility has appeared again and again in the Calvinistic camp. Antinomism's dirty head has protruded again and again to strike at the heel of the gospel of grace. And hyper-Calvinism is antinomism with reference to the preaching of the gospel, especially the imperative of the gospel, and with reference to the duty of men so addressed.

In its classic, developed form hyper-Calvinism denies that it is the duty of the church to preach the gospel of salvation to all men and to call all men to believe on Jesus Christ. The gospel is to be preached only to the elect, and only they are to be called to faith. The grounds put forward for this position are the doctrines of election, limited atonement, and irresistible grace, that is, Calvinism. Hyper-Calvinism also denies that it is the duty of every sinner without exception to believe on Jesus Christ. Only the regenerated elect is required to believe. The ground for this position is supposed to be the doctrine of total depravity, that is, Calvinism.

The English Congregationalist Joseph Hussey (1660-1726) taught this hyper-Calvinism. A preacher must preach a different message to unregenerated sinners from that which he preaches to the converted elect: "You must preach the Gospel of the kingdom to them: exalt Christ (that is, preach that Christ is a special king to crush gainsayers — DJE). Do this, then, when you do not preach the Gospel of the blood of Christ to them."[5] A preacher may not command all to repent and believe: "It is not our duty to preach the mere form of the command...."[6] As regards infidels and Jews, a preacher may only "set" them "to believe in Christ naturally." Somehow, a preacher indicates to unbelievers not that they should believe on Christ with true faith, for this is not their duty, but that they should believe in Christ with "natural faith," something, according to Hussey, that lies within their natural power.[7] All of this is set forth as if it were the Calvinistic repudiation of the Arminian offer.

Calvinism becomes the ground for a restriction of the preaching of the gospel, a silencing of the gospel call, and a denial of human responsibility. The very errors with which Calvinism has always been charged by its foes and from which Calvinism has always had to disassociate itself are here acknowledged as an integral part of Calvinism.

Even though such a fully developed, hardened hyper-Calvinism does not threaten, a Reformed church must guard against the subtle inroads of the hyper-Calvinist heresy with all vigilance. She must resist every manifestation of the spirit of hyper-Calvinism, for it is not the spirit of Reformed Christianity. To guard against hyper-Calvinism is peculiarly the urgent task of the Reformed church which, in keeping with the Reformed tradition, has rejected the Arminianism of the well-meant offer of the gospel. Against this church, a favorite wile of the father of lies is the antinomism of hyper-

---

5.   Joseph Hussey, *God's Operations of Grace But No Offers of Grace* (Elon College, N.C.: Primitive Publications, 1973), p. 87.
6.   Ibid., p. 153.
7.   Ibid., pp. 156, 157.

Calvinism. Although she may never become suspicious or fearful, a Reformed church must watch against hyper-Calvinism with the keen awareness that this evil, like the opposite evil of Pharisaism, is not far from her since it is ingrained in sinful human nature.

What are the manifestations of the spirit of hyper-Calvinism? How does this fundamental enemy of the gospel attempt to subvert the truth, ruin a church, and dishonor the God of grace?

One such manifestation is a minimizing of Christ's mission mandate to His church with an appeal to election as the guarantee that God will save His people. There need not be an outright denial of the mission calling of the church; it is enough that there be unconcern and negligence. The church sits on her hands. Arminianism's emotional motivation for missions, "Many will perish, who otherwise might have been saved," is in error; equally erroneous is hyper-Calvinism's cold defense of its failure to engage in missions. Indeed, God will save His elect, all of them, but it pleases God to save them by the preaching of the gospel. He has revealed this in His Word: "For I am not ashamed of the gospel of Christ: for it is the power of God unto salvation to every one that believeth..." (Rom. 1:16). "For whosoever shall call upon the name of the Lord shall be saved. How then shall they call on him in whom they have not believed? and how shall they believe in him of whom they have not heard? and how shall they hear without a preacher?" (Rom. 10:13, 14).

The Reformed faith has a lively knowledge of and healthy respect for the fact that the sovereign God is a God Who uses means, thus establishing and maintaining human responsibility. It knows God as a God Who gives men their daily bread in the way of their working at a job; therefore, the Reformed faith demands that men work and refuses to feed anyone who will not work. It knows God as a covenant God Who saves the children of believers in the way of believers faithfully rearing their children; therefore, the Reformed faith does not counsel parents to inaction but calls them to establish sound homes and good Christian schools. It knows God as a faithful God Who infallibly preserves every saint in the way of his diligent use of the means of grace in the church; therefore, the Reformed faith does not conclude from preservation to carelessness but exhorts believers to frequent the house of God every Lord's day, to hear the Word and receive the sacraments. Just so, it knows God as a God Who will save all of His chosen people in all nations in the way of calling them to Jesus Christ in faith by the gospel; therefore, the Reformed faith cannot recommend passivity or excuse negligence in the matter of missions but calls the church to go into all the world and preach the gospel to every creature, commanding all men everywhere to repent and believe.

To separate what God has joined together, to divorce God's decrees and purposes from God's means, is no honoring of God's sovereignty but a tempting of the Most High. "As the almighty operation of God, whereby he prolongs and supports this our natural life, does not exclude, but requires the use of means, by which God of his infinite mercy and goodness hath chosen to exert his influence, so also the beforementioned supernatural operation of God, by which we are regenerated, in no wise excludes, or subverts the use of the gospel, which the most wise God has ordained to be the seed of regeneration, and food of the soul. Wherefore, as the apostles, and teachers who succeeded them, piously instructed the people concerning this grace of God, to his glory, and abasement of all pride, and in the meantime, however, neglected not to keep them by the sacred precepts of the gospel in the exercise of the Word, sacraments and discipline; so even to this day, be it far from either instructors or instructed to presume to tempt God in the church by separating what he of his good pleasure hath most intimately joined together. For grace is conferred by means of admonitions; and the more readily we perform our duty, the more eminent usually is this blessing of God working in us, and the more directly is his work advanced; to whom alone all the glory both of means, and of their saving fruit and efficacy is forever due. Amen" (Canons of Dordt, III, IV/17).

Another betrayal of the spirit of hyper-Calvinism is embarrassment and hesitation, that is, fear, over giving the call "Repent! Believe!" and over declaring the promise "Whosoever believes shall not perish, but have everlasting life." This language is not suspect. It is not the language of Arminian "free-willism." It is pure, sound, biblical language. It is as much a part of the Reformed heritage as is the statement of divine, double predestination. We must take care that we do not concede precious elements of the gospel to the Arminians. Because they have seized on certain elements of the Scriptures, have wrenched them out of their proper setting, force them into the service of their false gospel, and, thus, wrest them to their own destruction, we may not abandon those elements. Rather, we must continue to honor them as part of God's revelation and must continue to give them their necessary place in the proclamation of the Word. There is no "Arminian text" in the Scriptures nor one Arminian word. No more than we renounce love because the "liberals" abuse it do we downgrade the external call of the gospel and slight the promiscuous publication of the promise because heretics construct a message of salvation by the will of man from a perversion of them.

If the fruit of the preaching of the gospel is that men, pricked in their hearts, cry out, "Men and brethren, what shall we do?" or that a Philippian jailor says, "Sirs, what must I do to be saved?" it is not in place, it is not typically Reformed, to launch into a fierce polemic against free will or to give a nervous admonition against supposing that one can do anything towards his own salvation. The answer to such questions, the Reformed answer, is "Repent, and be baptized every one of you in the name of Jesus Christ for the remission of sins...," and "Believe on the Lord Jesus Christ, and thou shalt be saved, and thy house" (Acts 2:38; 16:31).

Although ordinarily hyper-Calvinism is afraid to call the unconverted to Christ, there may even be a hesitation to preach the call to repentance and faith within the congregation. One feels uneasy about this as if this goes in the direction of "works" or the altar call. Then, a preacher does grave injustice to the Scriptures and great disservice to God's people. If he dares to preach on Matthew 11:28, the merciful Savior's tender call to the laboring and heavy laden with its precious promise of rest, the bulk of the sermon is controversy with the Arminian corruption of the text. Little is done with the comforting message of the text. The tender, urgent call to the laboring in the audience is never given. The audience goes home convinced that the Arminian interpretation is wrong but without having heard the gospel themselves.

The Reformed faith condemns, indeed despises, the altar call. It has bad parentage: Finney. It is bad theology: universal grace dependent upon the free will of the sinner. It is bad practice: the transforming of the inner, spiritual activity of the heart into an outward, carnal activity of the body. The Scriptures nowhere present repentance or believing as a matter of "coming to the front." Besides, no Reformed church has an altar. But opposition to the altar call does not in any way imply opposition to the call of the gospel to the spiritually laboring and laden sinner to come to Christ for rest. God forbid!

When hyper-Calvinism has developed somewhat, there is a failure, even a refusal, to preach the admonitions and exhortations of the Scriptures to the saints on the ground that good gospel preachers should not tell God's people what to do. At the very least, the admonitions and exhortations are not proclaimed with the sharpness, urgency, boldness, and freedom that obtain in the Scriptures. From this stage, it is but a little way to the disorder and license of open antinomism: "Let us sin that grace may abound."

How such a notion can be mistaken for orthodoxy is a mystery. How it can be mistaken for *Reformed* orthodoxy is a still greater mystery. The Scriptures abound with exhortations and warnings to God's people. Calvin, theologian of holiness that he was, is full of them. The Canons of Dordt expressly warn the Reformed pastor not to interpret sovereign grace as rendering admonitions and discipline unnecessary (III, IV/17). Luther, peerless defender of the gospel of grace against every encroachment of illicit law and glorious champion of justification by faith only, can be our teacher and guardian here:

> The churchly office of preaching is necessary not only for the ignorant who must be taught, for the simple and stupid populace and the youth, but also for those who well know what they ought to believe and how they ought to live, in order to awaken and admonish them

to be daily on their guard, not to grow weary
and listless, nor to lose heart in the battle they
must wage upon earth against the devil, their
own flesh and all vices. Hence St. Paul so
diligently admonishes all Christians that he
almost seems to be overdoing the thing, by
continually dinning it in their ears, as though
they were so ignorant as not to know it of
themselves or so careless and forgetful as not
to perform it without this telling and urging
them. But he knows full well that, although
they have begun to believe and are in that
state in which fruits of faith must appear, the
thing is nevertheless not so easily carried out
and brought to completion. It will not do to
think: "It is enough to have given them the
truth; when the spirit and faith are present the
fruits of good works will follow of
themselves." For while it is true that the spirit
is present and is willing, as Christ says, and
works in them that believe, it is likewise true
that the flesh also is present, and flesh is weak
and indolent. The devil, moreover, is not
keeping holiday, but seeks by temptation and
incitement to cause the weak to fall. Here you
dare by no means be negligent or indolent; as
it is, the flesh is too indolent to obey the Spirit,
nay it is strong to resist it, as Paul says in
Galatians 5:17. God, therefore, must deal
here as a good householder or faithful regent,
who has a lazy man-servant or maid-servant
or indifferent officials. (They need not be
actually wicked or disloyal.) He must not
think it enough to tell them once or twice
what to do, but must be constantly at their
heels and personally urge them on. So, too,
we have not reached the point where our flesh
and blood go leaping in pure joy and eagerness

to do good works and obey God, as the Spirit would gladly have us do and directs us to do. On the contrary, even though faith unceasingly urge and buffet the flesh, it scarce succeeds in accomplishing very much. What would be the result if this admonition and urging were omitted and one were to think, as many Christians think, "Well, I know of myself what I ought to do; I have heard it so many years and so often, and have even taught it to others, etc." I verily believe that if we were to cease our preaching and admonishing for a single year, we should become worse than heathen.[8]

The Reformed church rejects hyper-Calvinism, not because she hedges on her Calvinism at the last moment but exactly because of her Calvinism. Knowing her salvation as the sovereign, free, gracious calling of God in Christ, she burns with zeal for the glory of her God. In the love of her thankful heart, she desires that His great Name, Jesus, be published to the ends of the earth and that His good commandments be obeyed. God's grace in Jesus Christ has its sovereign way with her so that God's purpose in the calling of her is realized: "that ye should show forth the praises of him who hath called you out of darkness into his marvellous light" (I Pet. 2:9).

---

8. Quoted in M. Reu, *Homiletics* (Chicago: Wartburg Publishing House, 1924), pp. 159, 160.

Index to Scriptural Passages